Nature Walks
in Southern
New Hampshire

Distributed by The Globe Pequot Press, Inc.

Library of Congress Cataloging-in-Publication Data

Older, Julia, 1941—
    Nature walks in southern New Hampshire: an AMC nature walks book / Julia Older, Steve Sherman.
        p. cm.
    Includes index.
    ISBN 1-878239-35-X (alk. paper): $10.95
    1. Hiking—New Hampshire—Guidebooks. 2. Walking—New Hampshire—Guidebooks. 3. Nature study—New Hampshire. 4. New Hampshire—Guidebooks. I. Sherman, Steve, 1938– . II. Title.
GV199.42.N4043 1994
796.5'1'09742—dc 20   94-19606
                                                          CIP

The paper used in this publication meets the minimum requirements of the American National Standard for Information Sciences—Permanence of Paper for Printed Library Materials, ANSI Z39.48–1984.∞

**Due to changes in conditions,
use of the information in this book
is at the sole risk of the user.**

Book and Map Design: Carol Bast Tyler

Printed on recycled paper using soy-based inks.
Printed in the United States of America.

10 9 8 7 6 5 4 3 2   95 96 97 98 99

Nature Walks in Southern New Hampshire

An AMC Nature Walks Book

Julia Older
Steve Sherman

APPALACHIAN MOUNTAIN CLUB BOOKS
BOSTON, MASSACHUSETTS

Contents

Southeast New Hampshire
(East of the Merrimack River)

East Concord
Merrimack River Outdoor Education and Conservation

Nature Walks in

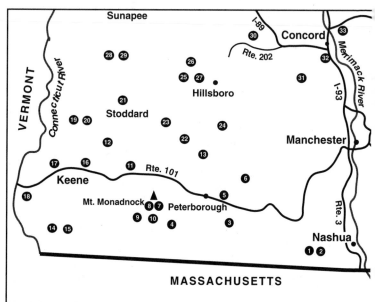

Southern New Hampshire

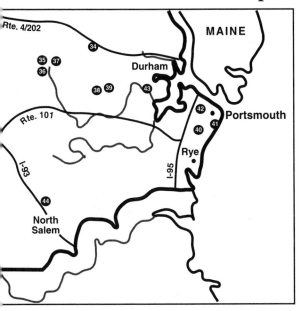

Introduction

NEW HAMPSHIRE offers an extraordinary array of rivers, brooks, mountains, valleys, woodlands, bogs, lakes, and ponds. The numbers are impressive: 40,000 miles of streams; 2,000 lakes and ponds; 182 mountains over 3,000 feet elevation; 86 percent of the state is forested. In that forest an active wildlife dwells—raptors, deer, mink, bobcat, moose, fisher, wild turkey, salmon, trout, and more.

But when "New Hampshire" comes to mind too many people think only of the White Mountains in the north. We hope that this book helps you think also of southern New Hampshire, where an equally wonder-filled backcountry—calm, safe, and reinvigorating—offers many rugged and graceful features.

Overall, New Hampshire offers a bonanza 12,000 miles of trails of all types and lengths—from quarter-mile footpaths to the developing 240-mile Heritage Trail, from the Massachusetts border to Canada. The walks in this book are short and sweet. Many are ideal for children. They include saunters along secluded beaver ponds, jaunts in highland meadows, strolls beside riverbanks, and ambles through pine forests. You don't have to carry a burdensome backpack or scramble over rough terrain, and only a few of these walks involve a vigorous hike up one of southern New

Hampshire's relatively modest mountains.

In addition, many of the trails are loops so you don't have to retrace your steps. Nearly all have directional blazes or are well marked with signs; the few trails that lack blazes are easy to follow. Many have picnic tables, rest rooms, and running water available, as well as visitor centers and guidebooks. A few have entrance fees, but they are generally nominal.

Locations

The walks selected for this book are all located south of Concord, New Hampshire. We've divided this area into two sections. The larger section extends west of the Merrimack River to the Vermont border. A smaller section stretches east of the Merrimack River to the Atlantic seacoast.

Walks in the southwestern region primarily are wooded and pass by many streams, marshes, ponds, and other wetlands. Since the southwest, like most of New Hampshire, is heavily forested, here you'll be walking through great stands of white pines, hemlocks, and among many other of the 74 species native to the state.

One of the most striking features of this area is Grand Monadnock (3,165 feet), a major regional landmark that stands above the forested plain. We've included two pleasant walks on this singular mountain as well as nearby rambles that feature great views of the popular peak.

East of the Merrimack River the land levels onto fields, pastures, and meadows until it tapers to the tidal estuaries of the 18-mile-long New Hampshire coastline. Less forested and more populated, this area still offers many inviting sites. Walks in this section take you along tidal basins, past farm pastures, and through dense tree farms. Bear Brook State Park, one of the largest recreational parks in the state, has miles of hiking and cross-country ski trails.

Society for the Protection of New Hampshire Forests (SPNF)

Several recommended trails pass through land under the auspices of the Society for the Protection of New Hampshire Forests. Begun in 1901, the "Forest Society" is now the largest and oldest conservation organization in New Hampshire. Through its work toward environmental education and land management, it was pivotal in establishing the White Mountain National Forest and many other important natural sites. Today the society owns land in 65 locations, varying in size from the 3,672-acre Monadnock Reservation in Jaffrey to the 4-acre Sutton Pines in Sutton.

A reason New Hampshire continues to offer such uncommon natural landscape for everyone to enjoy stems largely from the work of this home-based organization. Besides the trails throughout the state parks and forests that the Forest Society had a hand in preserving, trails in this book through SPNHF land include those in:

- McCabe Forest
- Shieling Forest
- Monadnock Reservation

- Peirce Reservation
- Warner Forest
- Merrimack River Outdoor Education and Conservation Area

Flora and Fauna

As you'll see, several of these trails and parks are named for beaver, otter, and bear. Bear do live in New Hampshire but are rarely seen. However, chances are favorable for spotting beaver, deer, porcupine, raccoon, gray squirrel, and other common animals.

Many of these walks skirt marshes, ponds, and rivers where you're also likely to see great blue herons, kingfishers, wood ducks, frogs, salamanders, and other wetland wildlife.

We've learned the advantage of taking a short, focused walk, rather than a longer hike—you see more. Why? Because you are walking slowly enough to spot animal tracks in the mud or bird nests in the trees, shy wildflowers beside brooks, or intriguing mushrooms on the forest floor. You are more aware of the sound of peeping tree frogs and hooting owls, more alert to the delicate smells of the backcountry. Your senses grow keen through observation and are sharpened by practice.

Dawn and dusk are the best times to walk if you hope to see feeding birds and animals. Otherwise, you can concentrate on the habits and habitats of flowers, ferns, weeds, mushrooms, and different conifers and deciduous trees. Nature discloses a constant array of fascinating discoveries.

In fact, many of the walks we've chosen are formal identification trails that describe tree, mushroom, and wildflower species. At "stations" along these trails you can often obtain an identification booklet that describes the local wildlife. Be sure to pick up an identification booklet if one is available (and return it at the end of the trail if requested). Taking along pocket-sized identification field books will also enhance your walk as well, leading to a richer knowledge of the outdoors.

As with all outdoor activities, remember to take a few precautions. Learn to identify poison ivy, poison oak, and poison sumac. Never consume a plant or berry you can't positively identify as edible. You'll be happy to know that virtually no poisonous snakes or spiders reside in New Hampshire, but ticks carrying Lyme disease have been found in all New England states. Because of deer ticks (the tiny mite that carries Lyme disease) and other biting pests, it's advisable to:

• wear long sleeve shirts, long pants, and high-top socks. Tucking pant legs into socks is added protection. Wearing light-colored clothing helps identify insects

• spray insect repellent around the ankles, wrists, and collar

• inspect all other parts of your skin after the hike

• remove any dark, rounded tick half-buried head first into your skin by removing it very carefully with tweezers without breaking off the head.

New Hampshire is graced with a bonus season—black fly season. It runs from mid-April to late June (when the mosquitoes take over). Your walk will speed up considerably if you're in the woods during this season. Nylon windbreakers with hoods help ward off the swarms of black flies hatching and hovering near ponds and marshes. Some people from this area stay indoors and some residents actually leave on prolonged vacations.

Mud season precedes black fly season and can be equally challenging. Good hiking boots or high waterproof shoes help. In fact, we recommend wearing high-quality boots in every season. New Hampshire is aptly nicknamed the Granite State, and no matter where you walk rocks crop up on the trails and pathways. Sturdy walking shoes or hiking boots with good ankle support give you safe traction and protection against slips and sprains, although the thick, deep lug soles can impact adversely on the gentler terrain.

Late fall is deer hunting season in New Hampshire. If you plan to be in the woods then, be sure to wear bright red or orange hats and coats so you aren't mistaken for deer by hunters. Check with town or state officials on the hunting seasons and postings.

Any walk takes energy, but more than mere fuel, snacks add to the enjoyment of any outing. Favorite standbys: apples, trail mix (almonds, raisins, jelly beans), and cookies.

Be sure to carry a lightweight canteen or bottle of water. Avoid carbonated soft drinks; you have to pack out containers and the carbonation can strain the body. Carry your own tap or bottled water rather than drinking spring or brook water, which may contain parasites.

Even on the shortest walks, we always carry a small knapsack for our guidebooks, water, snacks, binoculars, maps, a windbreaker, and a camera. You never know when you or others on the trail might want these supplies.

Whatever woodland you're walking in:

- respect the rights of landowners of private roads and property adjacent to a trail
- cut no standing trees or limbs, shrubs, or any other vegetation
- carry out what you carry in
- keep noise to a minimum for the benefit of other walkers and wildlife alike
- tread the trail softly.

Walking with Children

As parents know, discovering the world with children is, literally, a rejuvenating experience. Children refresh your encounter with the natural world as they spot tree frogs, shout at the sighting of red squirrels, tug at your arm to look inside rock ledges, or stare wide-eyed and drop-mouthed at a rainbow trout.

But let's face it. They can also tug at your arm in fifteen minutes to go home, whine for fifty yards for more trail food, and ask, "Are we there yet, are we there yet?"

Inevitably, nature walking with children requires adjustments. A few good principles are:

- go slowly
- enjoy following their interests
- remember that they have short legs
- a little information goes a long way

- anticipate quick energy depletion—half the trail accomplished means half the trail left to walk.

By all means, make nature walking enjoyable. Children are out to have fun and their naturally explosive interests and energy can be a delight to unleash.

Some of the best trails here for children include:

- Beaver Brook Association: Nesting Box Demonstration Trail
- Shieling State Forest: Boulder Trail
- Rhododendron State Park: Wildflower and Rhododendron Trails
- Ashuelot River Park (Keene): Ashuelot River Trail
- Surry Mountain Park: Beaver Lodge Trail
- DePierrefeu-Willard Pond Audubon Wildlife Sanctuary: Hatch Mill Pond Trail
- Elm Brook Park: Elm Brook Nature Trail
- Elm Brook Park: Everett Lake Dam Walk
- Silk Farm Wildlife Sanctuary: Turkey Pond Trail
- Pawtuckaway State Park: Tower Trail
- Odiorne State Park: Odiorne Point Trail ·
- Robert Frost Farm: Hyla Brook Nature/Poetry Trail.

How to Use This Book

Every natural area covered in this book has one or two walks with special appeal. Each walk has a separate identity. Although individual walks may be located in the same park or wilderness, the walks all have their own directions for getting to the trailhead and their own trail maps. First, we name the park or area, the nearest major town, and the acreage. Next, we give the name of the trail, its length, and the time for walking it. In addition, a one-line summary describes the character of the recommended trail as a quick reference to see if you'd like to try it. Of course, everyone walks in the woods at his or her own pace (usually about two miles per hour), and these times are meant only as approximations. The first paragraph of our narrative gives you a general description of the area. This is followed by brief directions for getting to the trailhead. A more detailed description of what you will see on the selected trail follows.

Joy of Discovery

We've walked all the trails in this book, some of them many times. In rare instances a trail must be rerouted or reblazed. For the most part, we have selected trails in well-established parks and preserves where additional information about the status of a trail is available.

May you enjoy these walks as much as we do. When we walk these trails, often we find a sense of euphoria overtakes us as the cares and stresses of twentieth-century living slip away. Lush woodlands, vivid panoramas, and the feeling of secluded wilderness contribute to ideal environments for nature walks in southern New Hampshire. We hope that, like us, the more walks you take the more you will discover.

Southwest New Hampshire

Beaver Brook Association
Hollis
1,730 Acres

Recommended walk: Nesting Box Demonstration Trail, 3/4 mile (loop), 1 hour 15 minutes

---

A self-guided tour of natural and man-made nesting areas for birds and small mammals.

Located only 45 miles northwest of Boston, the Beaver Brook Association's greenbelt of wood and water land offers plenty of choices for walks. Since the primary purpose of the Beaver Brook Association is education, you may meet up with a school class on a field trip or garden club learning about rock shrub plantings. Programs in forest, wildlife, and horticultural management are also available.

The demonstration trail focuses on the birds and small animals that benefit from man-made nesting boxes. It also draws the walker's attention to natural habitats preferred by certain species. Taking this trail won't ensure that you'll spot a kestrel or an eastern bluebird, but it shows the possibilities of attracting

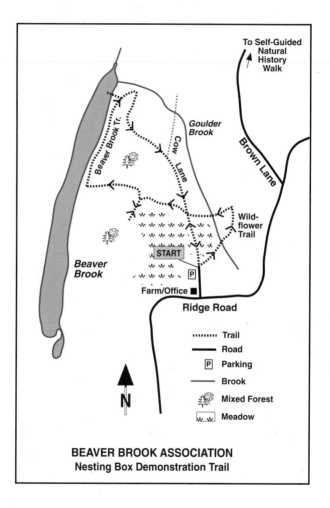

To Self-Guided Natural History Walk

Beaver Brook Tr.

Goulder Brook

Cow Lane

Brown Lane

Wild-flower Trail

START

P

Beaver Brook

Farm/Office ■

Ridge Road

.... Trail
──── Road
P Parking
──── Brook
🌳 Mixed Forest
🌱 Meadow

N

BEAVER BROOK ASSOCIATION
Nesting Box Demonstration Trail

birds through the setting out of nesting and breeding boxes. (You can even learn to make the nesting boxes yourself by contacting the trail's creator, Jason Stone, through the Beaver Brook office.)

Enter the trail at the Beaver Brook sign, to the right of the parking lot road. Here you can pick up a copy of a booklet that describes the trail through numbered stations. Walk a mowed swatch on the edge of the field and down into the wildflower area. At first, you will follow the well-marked Wildflower Trail. An introductory ledger on the left details some of the wildflowers in northern woodlands. Curve left onto the shortly overlapping Big Tree Trail and enter mixed hardwood and softwood forest where red-bellied (and

One of the many nesting boxes you'll see on trails in New Hampshire forests.

other) woodpeckers and black-capped chickadees like to nest (described at stations 1 and 2 in the booklet).

Turn left with the Wildflower Trail. You'll come to another ledger describing ferns. Cross a footbridge over Goulder Brook. On your left is the meadow you first crossed. Northern flickers, large yellow-colored woodpeckers with white rump patches, choose meadows and edge habitats for feeding and nesting (see station 3).

The Wildflower Trail jogs briefly to the right onto a dirt road (Cow Lane) and reenters the woods to the left. Follow green metal arrows.

Gray and flying squirrels (described at stations 4 and 5) nest in mixed forest such as this one. In late fall and winter you may see their huge circular nests of branches and dried leaves at the tops of oaks and hickories. Nesting boxes for squirrels are covered with a bottom layer of leaves to make them feel at home.

At the junction sign "Not a Ski Trail" turn left and walk to a large field. The meadow, beyond the stone wall on the left, provides nesting for eastern bluebirds, tree swallows, and American kestrel (stations 6, 7, and 8). Bluebirds like houses in the open and kestrels prefer edge forest habitat. Needless to say, the nest box opening is smaller for swallows and bluebirds. The high-flying kestrel nests ten to thirty feet above the ground; smaller birds prefer lower houses.

Backtrack to the "Not a Ski Trail" sign at the corner of the field and turn left into the woods, following green arrows through moist hardwood and conifer forest with rodents, frogs, and insects—perfect terrain for barred owls (station 9). You probably won't see or hear any owls in the daytime since these large-eyed, puffy-headed creatures are nocturnal; they wait out the daylight in other birds' deserted nests or burrows. They hoot and swoop on their prey at night when cover of darkness and sharp eyesight give them the advantage.

The trail descends a steep embankment to a large dead tree trunk. A nearby ledger explains that trees like this often are killed by porcupines that girdle the trunks with their gnawing. Like beaver, these large bristly rodents digest bark. Porcupine also adore gardens and apple orchards. Their varied diet also includes an occasional salt lick put out for deer. Leather harness and saddles containing salts add to their prandial pleasures. Porcupine use tree trunks, abandoned buildings, and rock caves as dens. Contrary to popular opinion, porcupine don't shoot their barbed quills. Only when an intruder or predator touches the bristly quills are specialized hairs released to pointedly penetrate the victim's skin.

Continue your descent through damp forest. Turn right onto the Beaver Brook Trail and walk along a marshy swale. Great-crested flycatchers (see station 10) nest in edge pines and hardwood trees near their watery landing ground. Pass through a corridor of lush green mountain laurel with glimpses to the left of large nesting houses for wood ducks and hooded mergansers (stations 11 and 12) in the marsh to the left.

At an orange dot cross-trail turn left and walk on planks to a wide bridge spanning the deepest water in this marshy area—an ideal place to observe life in Beaver Brook.

Return along the planking and follow a trail marked with orange dots a short distance until you reach the road (Cow Lane). Across the road a sign points to Leatherwood Trail but turn right onto Cow Lane and follow it back to Maple Hill Farm, about a third of a mile, walking through mature mixed and coniferous forest. Nuthatches and red squirrels (stations 12 and 13) frequent this type of woodland throughout New Hampshire.

In 1990 Beaver Brook Association earned the Wildlife Stewardship Award for Wildlife Habitat Improvement cosponsored by the New Hampshire Fish and Game Department and the University of New Hampshire Cooperative Extension Service. As you become acquainted with the property and programs of this nonprofit organization, you will understand why. Their aims are high, and their dedication to this vast parcel of land and its wildlife are apparent everywhere.

Getting There

Take exit 6 west off Route 3 in Nashua and continue on Route 130 west to Hollis. Turn south on Route 122 and drive 1 mile to Ridge Road. Turn west (right) onto Ridge Road and drive 1 mile to Maple Hill Farm, the office for Beaver Brook Association at 117 Ridge Road. The parking lot is located behind the farmhouse.There is no charge for exploring the 30 miles of trails and roads. However, some of the maps and guide booklets are sold for a nominal fee.

Beaver Brook Association
Hollis
1,730 Acres

Recommended walk: Self-Guided
Natural History and Forestry Trail,
1 mile (loop), 1 hour

An outstanding identification trail through 90 sites and several microenvironments.

You'll get the most from this wonderful identification trail by buying the association's informative, thirty-nine-page booklet explaining ninety marked sites. The booklet is available at the main office for a nominal fee. Its subtitle tells you what to expect: "Geology, Ecology, Forest and Wildlife Habitat Management, Conservation Practices, Land History, Wildflower and Tree Identification Or Across 600 Million Years on One Linear Mile!"

A one-mile drive from the Nesting Box Demonstration Trail (see page 1), the Natural History and Forestry Trail begins at a sign behind the farmhouse residence in the north section of the Beaver Brook Association's land. It leads into the woods. You'll walk through several terrains, including an enchanting cliffside section through evergreens. Identification markers (metal prongs with flat, numbered surfaces) corre-

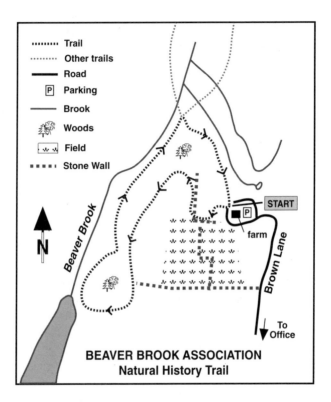

Trail
Other trails
Road
P **Parking**
Brook
Woods
Field
Stone Wall

N

START

P

farm

Brown Lane

To
Office

BEAVER BROOK ASSOCIATION
Natural History Trail

Beaver Brook

spond to the numbers and information in the booklet. The markers are stuck into the earth at trailside.

At the outset, as you walk by an old orchard, a stone wall invites you to step across 600 million years—the geologic history visible in the wall, which is comprised of a variety of sedimentary, metamorphic, and igneous rocks formed or deposited here over the ages. The darker, layered sedimentary stone results from the compression of silt, beginning 600 million years ago, in an ancient sea that once covered southern New Hampshire. Metamorphic rock was formed about 385 million years ago by tremendous continental pressures. Probably formed at the same time as the metamorphic rocks, the lighter-colored igneous rock in the wall formed from molten magma and contains visible crystals.

As you move deeper into the woods, notice examples of the three basic stages of forests. The pioneer or initial stage is heralded by fast-growing birches and aspens. Soon the longer-lived white pine, red maple, black birch, and oaks take over in the intermediate stage. Trees that can grow in the shade of others form the climax stage—sugar maple, American beech, and eastern hemlock (the longest-lived of native New Hampshire trees).

As you continue along the trail, markers point out not only trees and shrubs but also the drilled holes of yellow-bellied sapsuckers, which like tree sap, and the elliptical holes of pileated woodpeckers, which favors carpenter ants.

The trail curves around to the left and then downhill to marker 31 along the edge of a cliff that falls away to the right side of the trail. The air turns moist and cooler. This microclimate results from a slope facing northwest away from the sun. At marker 36, about halfway down the cliff, the power of a white pine splits a fissure into siltstone bedrock. As a seedling it took root in a small crack filled with nutrients.

White birches at Beaver Brook. Local Native American tribes used white birch bark to line their canoes and to weave baskets.

Descending a series of log steps, the trail flattens onto an ancient glacial floodplain 100 feet below the ridge top you just crossed. In this section, examples of managed and unmanaged forests demonstrate how white pine woodlands can be improved to produce well-formed trees and timber. The white pine around you is one of the most valuable timber trees in the world, prized for its fast growth, capability of reproducing in shade, and high-quality soft wood. The managed, right side of the trail shows how thinning out of poorer, obstructing trees allows other trees to grow taller and larger by letting in more sunlight. Pruning also increases the value of a tree by reducing the number of knots in the trunk (dead branches form the knots).

Cross a dirt road directly to marker 51 and traverse the pine forest floor where the trail turns right and passes mountain laurel shrubs at marker 53.

Follow the trail around the edge of an open beaver pond and beaver meadow. After a five-year stay, beaver left the pond in 1972. They returned for a time but abandoned the pond again. Beaver meadows are welcome for the edge effect they produce for wildlife, particularly nesting waterfowl—black ducks, wood ducks, hooded mergansers, Canada geese, and mallards.

The trail turns back into the woods. Shortly thereafter you recross the dirt road, then pass the base of the cliff you walked along the top of earlier. In this area hemlocks and white oaks compete for survival: Because they are longer-lived and more tolerant of shade, the hemlocks will win, but only if the chewings of porcupine, beaver, and gypsy moths don't weaken or kill them. As deciduous trees, oaks can grow back leaves in a season but the hemlocks can't.

Below the cliff is piled natural talus—ledges and rocks broken off from erosion and ice expansion. Talus, with all its angled rocks and hiding holes, makes good porcupine dens. These large rodents don't hibernate but instead eat hemlock twigs in winter, keep sheltered in the rocks, and use nearby Beaver Brook for their water supply.

Follow the cliff edge as the trail veers left then follows the road again. Turn right at a crossroads, then in a few yards turn right again and follow the trail uphill. Markers here identify good examples of sugar maple, beech, and American hornbeam (also called blue beech or ironwood). As you walk uphill, look on your right for the reddish tint of the straight and narrow trunks of a red pine plantation. Continue straight on the road to the end of the trail, about 100 yards.

Getting There

Take exit 6 west off Route 3 in Nashua and continue on Route 130 west to Hollis. Turn south on Route 122 and drive 1 mile to Ridge Road. Turn west (right) onto Ridge Road and drive 1 mile to Maple Hill Farm; the office for Beaver Brook Association is at 117 Ridge Road. There is no charge for exploring the 30 miles of trails and roads. However, some of the maps and guide booklets are sold for a nominal fee, including the 39-page booklet for the Self-Guiding Natural History and Forestry Trail. To reach this trail from the office, backtrack east on Ridge Road about 0.5 mile and then turn to the left at an island triangle onto Brown Lane. Follow Brown Lane, which is a dirt road, 0.5 mile to a farm building complex that is part of the association.

Wapack Trail
New Ipswich
21 Miles

Recommended walk: Wapack Trail/
Barrett Mountain Section, 1 mile,
45 minutes

---

*A sample mountaintop on this 21-mile summit trail that
stretches from Ashburnham, Massachusetts, to Greenfield,
New Hampshire.*

The name of this trail comes from the "Wa" of Mount
Watatic at the southern terminus in Ashburnham,
Massachusetts, and "pack" from North Pack Monadnock at the northern terminus in Greenfield, New
Hampshire. When the trail opened in 1922, it was
considered the first interstate footpath in the northeast
(work on the 2,100-mile Appalachian Trail began the
same year and was completed in 1937). Spearheaded by
Marion Davis, Frank Robbins, and Allen Chamberlain,
who later became a president of the Appalachian
Mountain Club, the Wapack Trail soon became a very
popular hike in the 1930s and 1940s before disregard set
in during the next two decades. But when walking the
woods regained widespread interest in the late 1960s
and 1970s, the Wapack once again enjoyed favor. In
1980 the Friends of Wapack was organized, and the
volunteer group gradually upgraded the trail with land

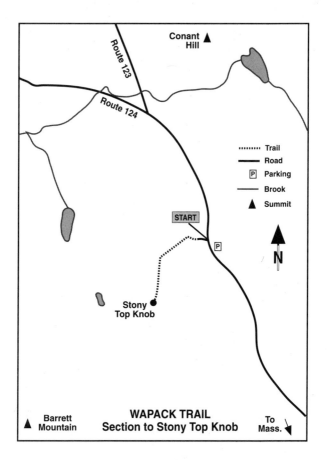

Route 123

Conant
Hill ▲

Route 124

········ Trail
━━━━ Road
P Parking
─── Brook
▲ Summit

START

P

N

Stony
Top Knob

▲ Barrett
Mountain

WAPACK TRAIL
Section to Stony Top Knob

To
Mass. ↓

protection and publication of a trail guide and history of this beloved footpath.

For the most part the Wapack Trail follows a skyline route, encompassing Watatic, New Ipswich, Barrett, Temple, Pack Monadnock, and North Pack Monadnock mountain summits. This short section offers unobstructed high elevation views without requiring too much exertion. The climb to a minor peak preceding Barrett Mountain is graded and relatively easy. The dark green spruce forest lends a definite flavor of northern exposure and deep alpine woods.

The Wapack Trail uses yellow triangular blazes and rock cairns to direct hikers over the mountains. Cross-country ski trails intersect and wind in and out this forested country. Sometimes as many as three different blazes are located at junctions, so double-check for the triangular Wapack blazes from time to time to keep on track. Hiking boots are in order because of the rocky, often wet terrain.

From the trailhead, scale a steep bluff leading to a well-trod narrow path lined with delicate brown-tinted wood ferns and fragrant short-needled spruce trees. If you run your fingernail gently down the stipe (stem) of the fern, you'll be able to tell it's a wood fern from its slight grooves.

Cross a dirt road and keep climbing. After about 0.25 mile you will come to a fork and continue forward. An intersecting trail leads north to the Windblown Ski Area. Walk through mixed hemlock and hardwoods dotted here and there with shiny green-leafed mountain laurel bushes that bloom pink and white in the early spring. The path widens and lazes up and down over small hills for a short distance. Make a sharp left at the Wapack sign tacked to a birch (another trail continues straight). Watch your step as you climb the last 0.25 mile to a bald spot surrounded by a tonsure of spruce, white pines, and classic white birch with peeling bark, also called the paper or canoe birch that Native Americans used to build canoes. Called Stony Top (not to be confused with another "Stony Top" south of Barrett Mountain), this bald spot is a lower summit but provides some long-distance views toward southern peaks in New Ipswich. This is a good stopping place. Barrett Mountain, about one mile farther south, offers limited views with dense, close-in forest walking. Here, you have a chance to loll on an open ledge and take in the expansive sea of green and the bewitching peaks encompassed by this long trail. Although the bald spot has partially grown in, with trimming it could offer a 360-degree observation area. Still, a few telescopic views on a clear day when the mountains seem especially close spark dreams of walking the entire 21 miles.

In spring alpine-type wildflowers such as cinquefoil, trillium, and wood lilies proliferate on the higher rocky, sunny slopes. And in fall the maples and birch blaze in bright orange, red, and yellow. The Wapack Trail passes by old homesteads and cellar holes, crosses the Massachusetts/New Hampshire border, and crosses the Boston Post Road first constructed in 1753.

Volunteers from the Friends of the Wapack maintain the trail, keeping brush cleared, blazes painted, and erosion in control. A complete Wapack Trail Guide and map may be purchased from Friends of the Wapack, P.O. Box 115, West Peterborough, N.H. 03468.

This small section of the 21-mile Wapack Trail overlooks Barrett Mountain to the south.

Getting There

From U.S. 101 east of Peterborough, N.H., turn south onto Route 123 toward Sharon and New Ipswich. Go 0.7 mile past the junction where Routes 123 and 124 meet. A granite marker and small sign on the right of Route 123 designate the Wapack Trail. Park on the shoulder of the road or at a cleared dirt parking area across the road. The Wapack Trail to the north leads to Conant Hill and Kidder Mountain. But look for the trailhead leading southwest. It starts 20 yards or so from the Wapack granite marker on a dirt drive with a sign reading "Wapack Road." The entire walk is on private land; please stay on the trail and do not litter.

Annett State Forest Wayside Park

West Rindge
7 Acres

Recommended walk: Black Reservoir
Pond Trail, 1/2 mile, 45 minutes

---

*A short forested walk to a gem of a pond in an extensive
necklace of lakes and reservoirs.*

This tiny pond is a secluded delight. Small, quiet, and
completely encircled with trees, Black Reservoir surprised us for how much it offers for so little effort. It's
part of the 1,300-acre Annett State Forest, given to the
state by the Governor's Councilor, Albert Annett of
Jaffrey.

To reach the pond at the Wayside Park, begin on
the left side of the rest rooms at the center rear of the
parking lot. A "Pond Trail" sign identifies the path.
Right away you enter a high and open hemlock and
beech forest. Follow the blue plastic blazes nailed to tree
trunks as you descend an easy, gradual trail through a
shallow ravine. In a short time, you'll see the pond
water sparkling through the woods. The trail leads
directly to the center point of the pond's southern edge.

When we first visited the pond, the bases of an
extraordinary number of trees along the water's edge

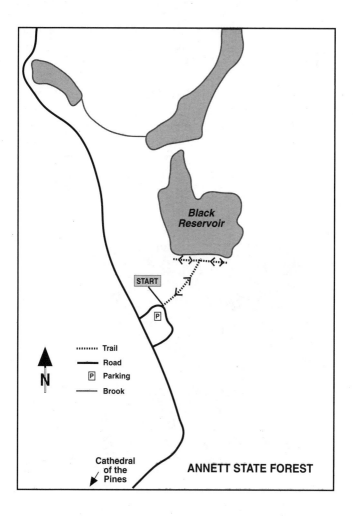

Black
Reservoir

START

P

.... Trail
——— Road
P Parking
——— Brook

N

Cathedral
of the
Pines

ANNETT STATE FOREST

showed the characteristic beveled marks of beaver teeth. Some hemlock and beech were chewed halfway through; others had only their bark eaten away. The diligence and strength of beaver are impressive for the size of trees they can fell. Larger trees supply them with smaller branches and twigs to construct dams and lodges. Beavers gnaw not only to eat and build houses but also to wear down their front teeth, which grow throughout a beaver's life. A beaver tooth is sometimes larger than a curved index finger. In addition, the teeth are anchored deeply into their jaws to give them power and long-lasting sturdiness. Here you see the remains of many beaver-worked trees.

This pine is in the process of being gnawed by beaver. After felling the trees, the beaver will use the branches to construct their dam.

From where the main trail meets the pond, turn left to take a footpath that follows the contour of the hillside for nearly 0.3 mile to the west corner of the pond. You'll pass low bunchberries with their bright red berries and low-bush blueberries, ripe and winey in August. Good examples of summer wildflowers also grow along the water edge, including pickerel-weed with its purplish blue spikes wrapped in dark green leaves, the low-spread golden thread (similar to shiny, oval, deep green wintergreen leaves but with a whitish centerline), Indian cucumber, and trillium with their bright red or purple berries on a central stem. In late afternoon especially, flycatchers—true to their family name—swoop over the water to catch insects on the wing. The gray eastern phoebe flycatcher is readily identified by the constant flick of its tail as the small, watchful bird sits on branches and vines.

Backtrack along the pond edge trail to the main trail. You can take a similar pond footpath to the right, with more impressive signs of beaver work but not as many wildflowers. Return to the parking lot on the blue-blazed Pond Trail.

Getting There

From U.S. 202 in West Rindge take Route 119 east uphill; pass the sign for Rindge Center on the right. In about 0.5 mile turn left at the sign for the Cathedral of the Pines. Drive 1.5 miles to the Cathedral and continue almost 1 mile farther to the Annett State Forest Wayside Park on the right.

Shieling State Forest
Peterborough
45 Acres

Recommended walk: Boulder Trail,
1 1/2 miles (loop), 1 hour 45 minutes

---

*A multifaceted, enjoyable walk through an intriguing range
of sites with monolithic glacial boulders.*

Well-designed and easily walked, this varied trail
winds through a forest with a broad range of fascinating sites for its relatively small acreage. The forest was
donated to the state in 1980 by Elizabeth Yates McGreal,
a prolific, well-known writer and resident of Peterborough for many years. The clearly marked trail was con-
ceived for educational outings through inspiring woodland. It is a fine introduction for children to the variety
of nature. In fact, one day we met two families we knew
having a good time seeing the old trees, meandering
Dunbar Brook, giant glacial erratic boulders, a rock
quarry, a wildflower garden, and other sites.

Begin from the meeting room and office building
next to the parking lot. The Boulder Trail begins at the
edge of the woods across a small field. Walk down
four brick and stone steps and into a red pine (Norway pine) plantation slanting downhill. Follow white
blazes to the bottom of the hillside and along a stone
wall to a footbridge over Dunbar Brook. From the

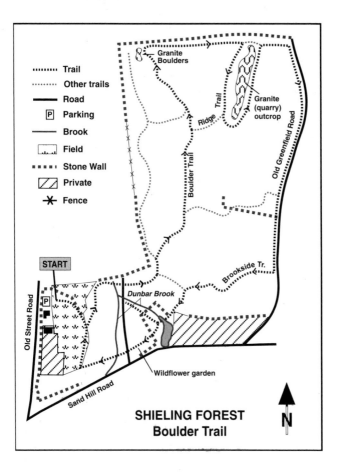

Legend:
- ········· Trail
- ·········· Other trails
- ▬▬▬ Road
- P Parking
- ──── Brook
- Field
- ■ ■ ■ ■ Stone Wall
- Private
- ✳ Fence

START

Granite Boulders

Ridge Trail

Granite (quarry) outcrop

Boulder Trail

Old Greenfield Road

P

Old Street Road

Dunbar Brook

Brookside Tr.

Wildflower garden

Sand Hill Road

SHIELING FOREST
Boulder Trail

N

footbridge continue straight ahead through a clearing with a picnic table on one side of the trail, a half-trunk bench on the other.

At a Y junction after you reenter the woods, bear to the left on a wide trail for a short distance. Then bear to the right at a second Y. Here the signpost for Boulder Trail directs the way up a slight incline. The wide trail continues through tall, mixed, open woods, including nearly 100-foot white pines. These hefty pines, identified partly by their long needles five to the bundle, were especially prized for ship masts by the British in colonial years. Scouts scoured New Hampshire for the best white pines and reserved them for the Crown, attaching severe penalties if cut by local colonists. Today many roads in the state are still called King's Highway or Mast Road and once were used to haul white pine trunks to Portsmouth on the Atlantic seacoast.

A short distance farther the pines give way to a cluster of maples in an old sugar grove. The old sugarhouse once situated here has since disappeared and many of the giant maples were destroyed when the well-remembered hurricane of 1938 swept through the state. Before this disaster, about 100 gallons of syrup a year were produced here; some maples still survive. Considering that the average ration of forty gallons of tree sap yields one gallon of syrup, an extraordinary amount of sap was collected. Supplying cordwood for the fire to boil off the sap water was an industry in itself.

At this cluster of maples you may see a Northern Tooth shelf mushroom on a tree's lower trunk. These hard beige layers of fungus look interesting but threat-

The Northern Tooth fungus, common in Shieling State Forest, feeds on the heartwood of maple trees.

en the life of the maple by eating into the thin, life-force cambium, whose cells divide to form wood and bark.

When you come to a connecting path on the right, continue straight on the Boulder Trail. As you do, the predominant maples yield to a stand of hemlocks, shallow rooted and short-needled. In quiet woods, as these are, falling hemlock needles sound like delicate rain hitting the forest floor. This hemlock section is a deer-yard. In winter when the snow is heavy, the thick canopy of hemlocks prevents much of the snow from reaching the ground, inviting deer to stay and use the area for cover.

When you reach the next junction (with the Ridge Trail, entering on the right) remain on the Boulder

Trail straight ahead. Another junction with a connecting trail to the left comes up soon; continue straight ahead through these pleasant woods. Suddenly, through the trunks and downhill slightly to the left, The Boulders appear. These two dramatically posed granite behemoths are startling glacial erratics left from the Ice Age 18,000 years ago. The force of glacial sheets ripped this huge chunk from the Mount Ascutney area in Vermont and shoved it here. Originally, the two parts were one, but nature split them in half; heat, cold, corrosive rain, and expanding frost cracked them first, then plant roots further separated them.

Turn right at The Boulders and follow the trail along a low stone wall. When you reach the Ridge Trail signpost, turn right. You are going to follow an oval loop around an old granite quarry. Toward the bottom of the oval, Ridge Trail diverges to the right. Keep left to stay on the oval. Descend slightly around the back side of the quarry. Large blocks of granite (identified by their drill holes) were quarried here during the eighteenth and nineteenth centuries. Below the quarry the trail passes through a wonderful stand of American beech, lighting up the woods with silvery tree trunks and high crowns of translucent leaves.

When you reach the stone wall again, turn right downhill. In a few yards turn right again onto the Old Greenfield Road, a shaded dirt road bounded by a low stone wall on the left. Continue on the road past a breach in the wall on the left and past a connecting trail farther on the right. After a slight down slope, turn right at the marker post onto the Brookside Trail, which leads you through remains of white pine stumps. This area was logged decades ago but now white pine, red maple, and red oak have returned. Some rich-looking yellow birch grow here as well.

At a T junction, turn left and step across a stone wall into the Elizabeth Yates McGreal Wildflower Garden, designed by the Peterborough Garden Club. This compact, charming garden beside Dunbar Brook grows at the former site of a grist mill. We thoroughly enjoyed winding around the circular paths and matching the identification markers to the myriad plants. You'll see maidenhair ferns that grow in a semicircular pattern with a dark stem on the fern frond, spicebush, interrupted fern, royal oats, and about ninety varieties of wildflowers, shrubs, ferns, mosses, and ground covers.

A picnic table on the other side of a footbridge over a lilliputian pond makes a relaxing spot for a snack or lunch break.

From the bridge, keep left on the wide path that guides you through the red pine plantation again. Immediately before you cross another footbridge, notice the red brick fragments lying about. Before the American Revolution and into the late nineteenth century, the brick-making industry helped to develop the town of Peterborough. The Hadley family brickyard, located on this site, sold a thousand bricks for three dollars in the 1870s. Many long-standing buildings in Peterborough were built from Hadley bricks, including the old schoolhouse on Middle Hancock Road and the Unitarian Church on Main Street.

Cross another small footbridge, walk up a slight

This rock-lined trail leads to a high meadow in Shieling State Forest.

hill, and climb a few steps to the cleared field. Skirt the woods back to the trailhead and cross the field to the parking lot.

Getting There

Driving east on Route 101, just outside of Peterborough at the yellow blinking light, turn left onto Route 123. Drive 2 miles north on Route 123. The Shieling Forest parking lot is on the right, prominently marked by a large sign.

Greenfield State Park

Greenfield
400 Acres

Recommended walk: Hogback
Pond Trail, 1 1/4 miles (loop), 1 hour

An isolated pond and marsh trail away from the crowds of this popular family-oriented park.

Greenfield State Park is an engaging site well designed in separating from each other the areas for tent camping, RV camping, picnicking, swimming and canoeing on Otter Pond, and especially nature trail walking. The predominantly evergreen forests on soft rolling hills are well maintained and invite carefree walks in the woods.

The first part of the Hogback Pond Trail leads you to an open-sided, irregular-shaped pond. The last half guides you through airy woods on an effortless path. The trail is located far from any of the noise from the 252 campsites and swimming beach.

Begin by driving straight into the park, curve around the big office parking lot, pass the toll booth, and continue straight ahead to the "Dead End" sign. Turn right at campsite 247. The trailhead is located next to this campsite and is clearly marked as a hiking and cross-country ski trail. Park here by the side of the road.

The first section of the trail follows a wide berth under red pines with their scaly, deep-cut, reddish

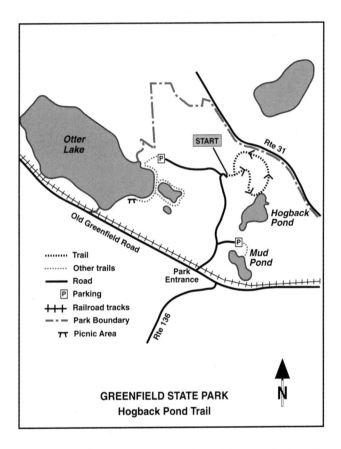

GREENFIELD STATE PARK
Hogback Pond Trail

Trail map legend:
- .... Trail
- .... Other trails
- —— Road
- P Parking
- +++ Railroad tracks
- —·— Park Boundary
- ᴛᴛ Picnic Area

Otter Lake

START

Rte 31

Hogback Pond

Mud Pond

Old Greenfield Road

Park Entrance

Rte 136

N

bark; lots of young water oaks with rounded, soft-edged leaves grow along the path. At the cross-trail take the right fork. You'll see a sign for Hogback Pond Trail in a few yards. (To the left is the less-interesting

North Loop and straight ahead is an old tote road used for carrying out timber.) Follow blue plastic blazes nailed to tree trunks. After winding briefly through a spread of mixed woods, veer right, downhill, at a Y junction. Ignore two connecting trails entering on the left. Stay on the main trail as it flattens and widens. A pair of giant white pines tower over you on the left. On the right you soon approach a long stretch of marsh, grown in with gorse and extending from this shallow floor bottom into Hogback Pond up ahead.

Gnarled-branch pitch pines grow beside the edge of the gorse, oddly beautiful with their unpredictable shapes. The now-sandy trail indicates the predominant soil here. So do the trees: pitch pines do well in moist, sandy earth while many other trees don't. The "pitch" refers to the high content of resin in these maverick pines, good for their long-burning cones and logs but not much else. This moist area also is conducive to scrub oak and low-bush blueberries.

The openness allows you to look ahead for waterbirds on the pond and approach them at nearly pond level without making noise and scaring them off. Several times we've seen great blue herons fishing in Hogback Pond. These spindly, four-foot-tall gray birds stalk and hunt with exotic deliberation, as if moving in T'ai Chi slow motion, stepping gingerly and silently. Then they lean forward close to the water and lock themselves motionless until a fish, frog, crawdad, or insect comes into prime range. Suddenly, with deadly accuracy, these patient herons release the energy behind their stiletto beaks and—the catch!

This wide, sandy trail passes a gorse-filled marsh on the way to Hogback Pond.

The trail meets the northern edge of the pond and curves left. Two short paths through the brush closer to the water. As you reach the end of the pond, trail blazes direct you to the left, but walk a few dozen yards around and slightly above the end of the pond to get a complete view at all of the rounded points and coves of this attractive, quiescent scene.

Reentering the woods, the trail funnels to a single-file pathway undulating slightly through luxurious woods and plants—from the symmetrically leafed bunchberry with its cluster of scarlet autumn berries to the sky-reaching evergreen white pines. Along this back stretch grow a generous sampling of head-high shrubs, including the highbush cranberry, identified by its three-tipped, maplelike leaf. Here we passed a sapling with a leaf that caught our attention—sassafras. The mitten-shaped sassafras leaf is unmistakable. Not all sassafras leaves grow this way but many do. What a delight. We hadn't seen sassafras, or savored its root beer aroma, since hiking the Appalachian Trail through the South. On Hogback Pond Trail we searched for other sassafras and found none. The sample we spotted grew beside the trail; we hope it's still there for you to enjoy and pass by too.

Keep an eye out for the Old Man of the Woods, also called the "pine cone fungus." This mushroom grows in moist, mixed woods and looks like a classic mushroom with a domed cap held by a slender stem. The telling difference lies in its scaly, darkish, shaggy look. The one we saw here looked like a burnt roasted marshmallow. They're edible, but unless you're expert in mushroom hunting, admire it from a distance.

Ahead, the trail crosses three dirt roads. Turn left on the third road. On a tree up high a small orange sign with an arrow says, "ST PK" (STATE PARK). This woodsy road leads straight back to the Hogback Pond Trail turnoff and the trailhead at campsite 247.

Getting There

From Route 101 in Peterborough, turn onto U.S. 202 and drive north about 2 miles. Turn right on Route 136 and drive about 6 miles toward Greenfield. Signs for Greenfield State Park are clearly marked.

Monadnock State Park
Jaffrey
5,000 Acres

Recommended walk: Wildwood Nature and White Dot Trails, 2 miles, 1 hour

---

A pleasant, booklet-guided nature trail on the way to Falcon Spring with cool, refreshing mountain water.

Grand Monadnock is a wonderfully singular mountain. Located in rural, wooded, southwestern New Hampshire, Monadnock is one of the most beloved and democratic mountains anywhere. At only 3,165 feet elevation, reaching the top is within the ability of nearly anyone—and the rewards are spectacular at this roadless peak. The broad, rocky summit overlooks a full-circle horizon, including all six New England states.

Many luminaries of the past have enjoyed Grand Monadnock. Ralph Waldo Emerson called it "the airy citadel." Nathaniel Hawthorne described Monadnock as "visible like a sapphire against the sky." Rudyard Kipling wrote that "Monadnock came to mean everything that was helpful, healing, and full of quiet." Native Americans before them knew it by several names, including "the place of the unexcelled mountain" and "mountain that stands alone." So dramatic did the mountain appear to early geologists that it became the prototype of the generic term "monadnock:

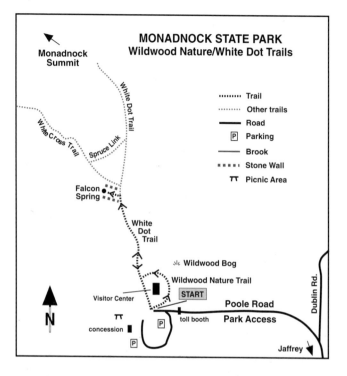

MONADNOCK STATE PARK
Wildwood Nature/White Dot Trails

Monadnock
Summit

White Dot Trail

White Cross Trail

Spruce Link

....	Trail
....	Other trails
▬	Road
P	Parking
───	Brook
▪▪▪▪▪	Stone Wall
⊤⊤	Picnic Area

Falcon
Spring

White
Dot
Trail

⚜ Wildwood Bog

Wildwood Nature Trail

START

Visitor Center

N

⊤⊤

concession ▪

P

toll booth

Poole Road

Park Access

Dublin Rd.

Jaffrey

a hill of resistant rock standing in the midst of a pene-plain."

Although crowds of hikers fill the White Dot Trail, we never tire of it because delicious, sparkling Monadnock water from Falcon Spring awaits us about 0.75 mile from park headquarters. To add an enjoyable beginning, walk around the Wildwood Nature Trail next to the White Dot Trail.

Booklets describing nature along the Wildwood Trail are located on a post a few yards beyond the ranger's cabin to the right of the visitor center after you pass the sign: "White Dot Trail to Falcon Spring, White Cross Trail, Cascade Link Trail." The nature trail is best walked in snowless seasons.

Thirteen identification stations are marked by numbers painted on stones along the trail. Follow the stone-lined trail about a third of a mile through the woods and along a bog. Walk through familiar white and yellow birches, American beech, white pines, and red spruce. Station 3 describes the geological signs of an ancient sea that layered sand and mud deposits here, creating sedimentary rocks. The inexorable crush of continental plates 400 million years ago folded these flat layers to create the crumpled terrain found today in this region. In fact, the entire mountain consists of folds of quartzite and schist, sedimentary layers hardened by intense heat and pressure. The Billings Fold, found on a southern cliff close to Smith Summit and White Arrow Trails near the peak, is well known. This fully exposed example of seven distinct layers was pressed by tremendous geologic pressure. The layers fold over each other like ribbon candy.

The Wildwood Trail also offers smaller and more delicate sights. At station 5 tiny pipsissewas grow in the rich, moist woods. The waxy white or pink flowers are fragrant and grow low to the ground with big-toothed, narrow, leathery leaves. Root beer extracts are made from pipsissewa. Follow the trail past the bog and eventually up a slight incline to cross two small wooden footbridges at station 11. At station 13 leave the guide pamphlet in the posted box so it may be used by others. A few more yards take you directly to the White Dot Trail. Turn right, and continue up the base of the mountain.

Despite the many thousands of people lured to Grand Monadnock over the years, the White Dot Trail remains relatively unspoiled. The trail is wide and worn but retains the clean sturdiness of a well-traveled and well-loved mountain path. It leads you through stands of birches, oaks, maples, and white pines. While

Here the trail separates from the White Dot Trail for the short turnoff to Falcon Spring on Grand Monadnock.

walking the trail is not too demanding, rocks, logs to prevent erosion, and thick tree roots take some effort now and then. Overall, the walk gives you an introductory taste of Grand Monadnock.

At the junction with Spruce Link Trail (leading to White Cross Trail and connecting trails to the summit) keep straight on the White Dot Trail. Not too much farther, a tall pine grows in the middle of the trail; at this point look on the left for a path bordered by stone walls to Falcon Spring. The spring is a short way from the main trail. Here you can rest, lean against the stand-up railing (good for those carrying backpacks), and refresh yourself with springwater running from a protected pipe, handy for filling canteens or cupping your hands for a good, long drink.

The spring is named after William Falconer, a full time watchman who lived in a cabin near here during the first part of the century. Every day he climbed to the summit shelter to look for fires. In 1911 the shelter became part of a watch system. The stone shelter was razed in the 1950s in favor of extended aerial surveillance.

From Falcon Spring the upward, sharper thrust of the mountain is easy to see. Return straight down the White Dot Trail to the parking lot. If the mountaintop beckons you, the White Dot Trail continues as the shortest of the five popular summit routes. It requires occasionally strenuous but manageable boulder climbing. Good shoes, snacks and water, and a windbreaker for unpredictable summit weather will make the trip more enjoyable.

Getting There

From Route 101 a quarter mile west of Dublin village center, turn south at the sign for Monadnock State Park. Drive 5 miles on this country road; going south it's called Jaffrey Road. Turn right at the park access road (Poole Road) and drive to the headquarters and parking lot. There is a nominal entrance fee for the park.

From U.S. 202 in Jaffrey south of the state park, turn northwest on Route 124 and drive about 3 miles to the hilltop of Jaffrey Center. Continue on Route 124 over the hill, and about 0.33 mile later turn right on Upper Jaffrey Road at the sign for Monadnock State Park. Drive about 2 miles and turn left at the park access road. Drive to the headquarters and parking lot.

Monadnock State Park
Jaffrey
5,000 Acres

Recommended walk: Old Toll Road,
3 miles, 2 hours

---

*A comfortable climb on a dirt road to dazzling views from a
clearing halfway up the mountain.*

Grand Monadnock gets its preeminence as one of the
most beloved mountains in the nation from its spectacular mountaintop views, accessible trails, and fascinating social and literary history. This walk follows the
footsteps of Henry David Thoreau, Ralph Waldo Emerson, Oliver Wendell Holmes, and other luminaries of
the nineteenth century who walked or road stage-
coaches up this road to the Half Way House hotel.

Considered the most-climbed mountain in the
country, Grand Monadnock always has someone on it.
Late summer and fall are the most popular months,
when you'll see walkers and hikers of all ages and
capabilities. Fortunately, the 40 miles of trails (five
main trails to the summit and many connecting paths)
disperse the crowds, except for Columbus Day weekend at the peak of autumn colors when all the trails
are crowded.

The road begins at a kiosk and a pass-through
gate with a sign reading, "Old Toll Road to White

Birches and pines line the Old Toll Road leading to the Half Way House clearing on Grand Monadnock.

Arrow Trail." This is the main route to the summit from the Half Way House clearing (many connecting trails from the clearing also eventually lead to the 3,165-foot summit). At the outset this pleasant walk is lined on both sides with American beech, white and yellow birch, and a few conifers. The climb is easy for the first 0.5 mile, where it flattens and veers to the right at a noticeable clump of white birch saplings.

Passing the birch saplings, the road angles a little steeper. When you walk up a short incline, look to the right for the Parker Trail, where a sign points the way

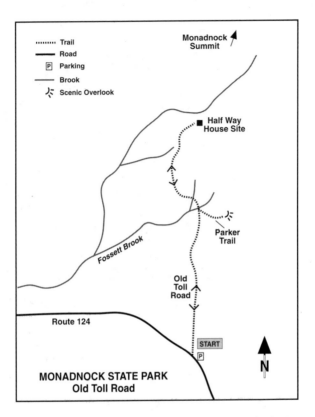

to the park headquarters. This junction is a little more than halfway to the old hotel clearing. A short side trek on the Parker Trail brings you to a ledge with a wonderful view south.

Once you've seen the view from the ledge, return on the Parker Trail to the Old Toll Road and turn right to continue uphill. Soon the road flattens again and passes through scattered hemlocks. Then the wide, dirt road tilts up slightly again. Watch on the right for a 20-foot exposed granite underlay, a slanted, flat section bordering the road. Notice the straight gouges in the rock where the tremendous pressure of moving glaciers scarred the granite. Another section of this ancient granite lies a few yards away.

When you hear the gurgling of water runoff channeled along and under the road, you're getting close to the clearing. In just over a mile from the trailhead, the road takes you around an upward bend where, to the right in the trees, you'll notice a private house, built here before the area was designated a state park. At the driveway entrance, turn left and continue up a wide, rocky route on the final short stretch to the Half Way House clearing. Before you reach the clearing, a narrow runoff from Moses' Spring trickles across the road.

Straight ahead is the rocky bald summit of Grand Monadnock. Human and natural histories intertwined to shape this singular mountain. A tangled system of timber and root cover allowed wolves and bears to proliferate and attack sheep herds on mountainside farms and fields. In retaliation local farmers and shepherds set fire in 1800 to drive the wolves out, but the fire got out of control, burned for two weeks, and completely destroyed the growth on the summit. The hurricane of 1815 finished the defoliation, creating what remains today—a rocky summit with an unsurpassed panorama. On clear days, mountaintops in all six New England states can be spotted from the summit.

The Half Way House clearing has its own wonderful views to the west, where you can see staggered horizons leading to the Green Mountains of Vermont. To the rear of the clearing on the right, where Moses' Spring flows at the base of a rock slab, an inscription reads: "Site of the Hotel known as the Mountain House and later as the Half Way House, 1886–1954."

Virtually nothing remains of the once-popular hotel, which in the mid-nineteenth century developed from a guest house into a three-story hotel serving as many as 100 guests. Vacationers trekked from Massachusetts, New York, and farther away to enjoy the glories of Grand Monadnock. The original Mountain

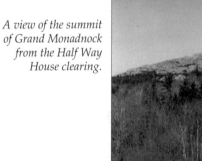

A view of the summit of Grand Monadnock from the Half Way House clearing.

House burned down in 1868 and was rebuilt, but when the Half Way House burned down in 1954 it was beyond restoration.

The clearing makes an ideal picnic spot. It's also a good starting point for exploring higher reaches. Many of the playful names for the trails leading from the clearing originated in the Half Way House days. To the immediate right of the clearing, a sign directs you to Hello Rock Trail, Point Surprise Trail, and the Thoreau Trail. (The Thoreau Trail is one of our favorites; it passes through good pine shade and the Emerson Seat overlook.)

At center rear of the clearing a sign marks these trails: Sidefoot Trail, Do Drop Trail, Noble Trail, Hedgehog Trail. To the far left of the clearing, and slightly in the woods, the White Arrow Trail angles to the summit. This trail is the oldest on the mountain, probably blazed in 1706. Here too begin the Monte Rosa and Fairy Spring Trails.

Return down the Old Toll Road to the parking lot.

Getting There

From Route 101 at Marlboro, take Route 124 southeast about 8 miles past Perkins Pond at the base of Grand Monadnock on the left and continue to the top of the hill. The parking lot for the Old Toll Road is on the left. From U.S. 202 in Jaffrey, take Route 124 northwest 2 miles through Jaffrey Center and continue over the hill for about 2 more miles. At the top of a hill the parking lot for the Old Toll Road is on the right. It's clearly marked.

Rhododendron State Park

16 Acres
Fitzwilliam

Recommended walk: Wildflower and
Rhododendron Trails, 1 mile (loop),
45 minutes

An enchanting stroll on a wildflower identification path and through the largest stand of rhododendron north of the Alleghenies.

The Fitzwilliam Garden Club came to the rescue of the hard-pressed park service in 1977 when most of this largest tract of rhododendron north of the Allegheny Mountains lay beneath fallen branches and trees from severe winter storms. The state gladly accepted their voluntary help, and in the intervening years the club has developed a lovely, well-maintained, and carefully marked wildflower trail in front of the entrance to the rhododendron thicket. The club also created a special brochure listing the flowers to be seen from April through September, a useful and artistic memento of your walk.

The trailhead is located near the pit toilets at the parking lot. Proceed straight along this wide, airy identification trail, soon bearing left. Continue until you reach the edge of the rhododendron thickets.

The 16-acre Rhododendron State Park is the largest stand of rhododendron north of the Allegheny Mountains.

Of course, in mid-July when rhododendron blossoms are at their peak, this 0.3-mile section is often overlooked. Staked wood plaques identify the more common woodland ground covers and wildflowers you're likely to see in southern New Hampshire. Three-leafed, dark green golden thread, partridgeberries, and Canada mayflowers, for example, may be identified by their blossoms in spring and by their leaves or berries in the fall. You may gently touch the soft silky needles of balsam as you pass or lean over to get a better look at a Christmas fern growing from a stump.

We've taken this short trail several times to refresh our memories and compare the structures of flowers such as the short, sharp-leafed starflower and taller

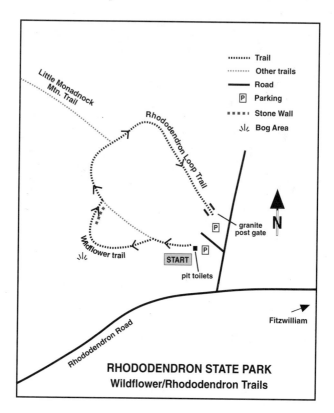

RHODODENDRON STATE PARK
Wildflower/Rhododendron Trails

whorl-leafed wood aster. The woods are cleared and open with an insulating cushion of pine needles. Nuthatches fly to and from trees, storing wildflower seeds for a snack later, and brown creepers look for insects in the fissures of the tree trunks. The mixed beech, maple, and pine forest is quiet and pleasant.

The trail leads you directly into the thickets, which tighten the path as you proceed. Whereas the identification trail evokes a spacious feeling, the rhododendron section sometimes crowds in like a jungle of thick, huge leaves and tangled branches and roots.

Rhododendron is a hardy deciduous shrub that grows luxuriantly in ravines and shaded moist forests with acid soil. Its tough roots form a tangle, and when the leathery leaves die they curl into tight brown scrolls that look like cinnamon sticks. In this park *rhododendron maximus,* commonly called rosebay, closes in on the trail in a few spots. From the rises, if you visit the park in mid-July, you may see the vibrant multiflowered blooms in spectacular profusion.

Rhododendron belongs to the "heath" family, a broad term related to the word heather. Shrubs of this family are evergreen with tough, scaly foliage and nodding, bell-shaped red, rose, lavender, or white flowers. Azaleas also are rhododendrons and come in an even wider variety of cone-shaped flower clusters. Because of their delicate constitution, however, azaleas don't do well in the harsh northern climate.

On the other hand, mountain laurel, which also belongs to the heath family, is quite at home in New Hampshire and blooms on roadside slopes and in mountain areas such as Monadnock in late May and June. Mountain laurel leaves are smaller than rhododendron leaves, and the shrub has pink and white flowers cupped and crenellated to catch spring rains. (In case you're wondering, mountain laurel isn't related to the bay laurel used as a seasoning for vegetable stews and other savory dishes.)

Rhododendrons shelter a variety of birds and animals. Ruffed grouse and flickers whir and rustle in the thick foliage. The massive root system keeps the soil loose and friable for skunks to dig holes looking for grubs and for squirrels to hide caches of acorns and beechnuts.

The trail loops through a stand of feathery hemlock, passing the turnoff to Little Monadnock Mountain and Metacomet Trails (see page 51). The trail terminus is grandly marked by two six-foot granite posts in the parking lot.

This park is a quiet haven we've returned to on those days when the world is too much with us. As Robert Frost wrote, "The woods are lovely, dark, and deep."

Getting There

In Fitzwilliam take Route 119 past the Fitzwilliam Inn 0.5 mile and turn right onto Rhododendron Road. The park entrance is about 2 miles on the right. Drive a very short distance past a private residence on your left to the free parking area.

Rhododendron State Park

Fitzwilliam

16 Acres

Recommended walk: Little Monadnock
Mountain Trail, 2 miles, 2 hours

A climb through forest to a dramatic view of nearby Grand Monadnock.

The top of Little Monadnock Mountain (1,883 feet) affords a magnificent view of Grand Monadnock (3,165 feet) to the northeast. Bring your camera along to capture the scene. Wearing sturdy hiking boots will also aid your climb. Gradually, you climb one mile up a well-marked trail with a few boulders to negotiate now and then.

From the granite post gate at the rear of the parking lot, follow the Rhododendron Trail 0.2 mile to the Little Monadnock trailhead (don't be confused by a sign for the Metacomet-Monadnock Trail, which comes in on the summit). Follow white blazes. The climb is gentle at first through a hemlock, white pine, and birch forest. Notice mica sparkling in the granite rocks of a stone wall. This silicate mineral of aluminum and potassium layered in thin sheets that shine and sparkle much like cellophane appears frequently in the gneiss and granite of this area. Cross a streambed and climb past a tumble of rough boulders

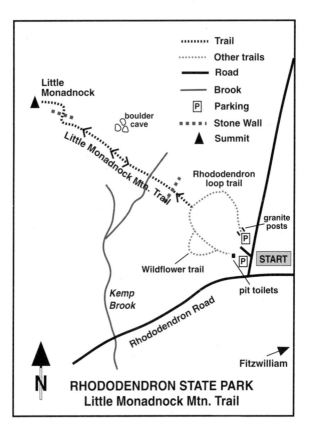

RHODODENDRON STATE PARK
Little Monadnock Mtn. Trail

in a mixed hardwood forest. A boulder cave about halfway up the trail gives the walker a place to lean or sit and look at the forest below. Children delight in the caves and recesses formed by these boulders.

About three-quarters of the way up the trail you follow another stone wall and eventually cross it. In the early nineteenth century much of the mountain was cleared for sheep pasture. The stone walls identified property and deterred livestock from wandering.

Each season changes the fragile treeless zone of these northern mountains. In spring, mountain cranberries and cinquefoil blossom from granite crevices. In summer, giant dragonflies flit over the summit like miniature helicopters and turkey vultures ride the thermals hunting for small prey. Early fall brings juniper berries and low-bush blueberries. Year-round, slate-colored white-tailed juncos hop in and out the scraggly grasses pecking at seeds.

Grand Monadnock as seen from the Little Monadnock Mountain Trail in Rhododendron State Park.

The top of Little Monadnock is approximately one mile from the first stone wall you crossed. Here you suddenly have a dramatic view of the south slope of Grand Monadnock. The Metacomet Trail enters a few strides on your left. The Metacomet-Monadnock Trail extends south from Grand Monadnock through western Massachusetts to Meriden, Connecticut; Little Monadnock Mountain is one of the many summits it crosses.

Invariably, the walk back down a mountain seems easier and quicker. Take care not to stumble on tree roots or rocks on the trip back into the forest. Once back down the mountainside, energy permitting, you may return to the parking lot via the Rhododendron Trail and the Wildflower Trail loop, adding an additional 0.5 mile. Or from the trail junction backtrack the 0.2 mile to the granite post gate where you started.

Getting There

In Fitzwilliam take Route 119 past the Fitzwilliam Inn 0.5 mile and turn right onto Rhododendron Road. The park entrance is about 2 miles on the right. Drive a very short distance past a private residence on your left to the free parking area.

Monadnock-Sunapee Greenway
Marlborough
51 Miles

Recommended walk: Eliza Adams Gorge
Walk, 2 1/4 miles, 1 hour 30 minutes

A scenic spillway and gorge on a section of this greenway stretching from Grand Monadnock to Mount Sunapee.

The Appalachian Mountain Club and the Society for the Protection of New Hampshire Forests have cosponsored protective agreements with landowners to perpetuate this footpath between Grand Monadnock and Mount Sunapee. The original trail connecting the two mountains in the 1920s fell into disuse after the destructive 1938 hurricane swept through New Hampshire. After some rerouting to the highlands, the greenway reopened in 1976 and now is a major addition to the trail system in the state. This walk is typical of some of the woods-and-water country the greenway traverses.

A broad way through mixed hardwood forest ends theatrically at this deep gorge with its spillway and dam. The spillway's water source, Howe Reservoir, is drained in early winter, so catch this showy spectacle from late spring through the fall foliage season (mid-October).

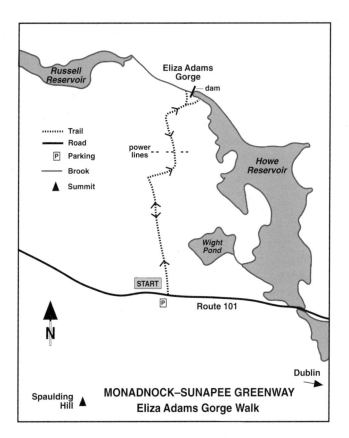

MONADNOCK–SUNAPEE GREENWAY
Eliza Adams Gorge Walk

Enter the trail behind the Girl Scout Camp sign and gradually climb the rocky, rutted dirt road through mixed conifers and birch. You'll follow the two-by-six-inch white blazes of the Monadnock-Sunapee Trail. Graceful, fountain-shaped sprays of chartreuse-colored ferns line tumbled stone walls on both sides of the road. The waist-high ferns with brown seed sacs midway up the stem are called interrupted ferns. Cinnamon ferns also grow in this area (look for little hairlike tufts at the base of the frond stem).

At a double blaze on your right, about one mile from the trailhead, turn right. A sign and arrow point to the nearby sign "M-S Trail" at a right angle to the road and into the woods. Amble steadily uphill on the wide path to a clear-cut area beneath power lines. This

This wide trail leads to a dramatic gorge on the 51-mile Monadnock-Sunapee Greenway.

clearing offers an excellent view downslope to the Howe Reservoir. As you reenter the woods notice the five-section trunk of a colossal, wide-girth yellow birch.

Ease downhill through a corridor of green-bark, slender goosefoot maples and tall, branchless oaks. Here the trail also serves as a bridle path so watch your step. This section of the trail is on private land; walkers are asked to respect this fact and be aware that they are guests.

About 0.13 mile from the reservoir, an offshoot path periscopes to the right down to the clear blue water near the reservoir outlet. Take this narrow footpath to have a look and say hello to the expansive lake. Then backtrack to the main trail and continue your walk with Howe Reservoir on your right.

The scenery changes from deciduous forest to conifers—a good setting for mushrooms. We happened on a five-inch chalky white Destroying Angel of the deadly *Amanita* family. This mushroom is easily identified by its double sheaths (below the cap and just above the ground where it protrudes from the soil). If you wish to examine mushrooms, don't touch them. Use a twig to uncover some of the stem for positive identifications. As the name of this mushroom implies, this and others of the *Amanita* family can be fatal when ingested.

Listen for the water spilling over the high dam to the stone-cluttered brook below (this brook connects to Russell Reservoir about 0.5 mile to the northwest). Careful steps across the rocks (especially slippery in spring) lead to the other side of the gorge. Here the Monadnock-Sunapee Greenway continues north to the town of Nelson. However, the pounding curtain of water over the dam upstages other scenes found in this section of the Greenway. Linger here, just below the dam, and enjoy the sights and sounds of the hemlock forest. To conclude your walk, backtrack and return to the parking area on Route 101.

Getting There

From Dublin drive west on Route 101. About 3.25 miles on the left pass a wayside park overlooking a small pond and Grand Monadnock. Continue another 0.5 mile. On the right look for the "Monadnock Wilderness Girl Scout Camp" sign and a steep dirt road. This is the entrance to the Eliza Adams Gorge Walk. There's enough room for parking (five to six cars) on the opposite side of Route 101 where the 51-mile Monadnock-Sunapee Trail descends from Grand Monadnock.

For further information about the Friends of Monadnock–Sunapee Greenway, a new non-profit club formed to maintain the 49-mile trail first laid out in 1921, contact Tim Symonds, guiding force of the club. He tells us the growing membership is revitalizing interest in this captivating trail winding through three states. Correspondence should be addressed to Tim Symonds, Friends of Monadnock–Sunapee Greenway, P.O. Box 164, Marlow, NH 03456.

Otter Brook Recreation Area

Sullivan

90 Acres

Recommended walk: Dave Shepardson Trail, 2 miles, 1 hour

A dirt-road walk along a reservoir lake to the top of a dam overlooking the recreation area.

While Otter Brook Dam is part of the flood control system for the Connecticut River basin, it also serves as a local recreation area. The entrance road descends from N.H. 9 into a shallow, partially forested river valley and passes alongside boulder-strewn Otter Brook lined with white pines and maples. Spacious picnic areas, a large open playing field, a small frog pond, sandy swimming beach, and a lake complete this modest-size, welcoming scene. It's an inviting place to walk.

The trail begins a short distance from the parking lot at a pass-through gate that blocks public car traffic. The relative openness of the dirt road, especially at the outset, allows a surprising array of wildflowers and shrubs to flourish in the sun. This pleasant walk will delight flower lovers of all ages.

Along the first half mile—open, straight, and shoreside—milkweed grows abundantly. Their broad, thick leaves are a good clue to identification, but in

Silk from milkweed pods was used by early settlers for stuffing pillows.

late summer the oval seedpods (that earlier were pink or red flowers) are easy to recognize. Children like to pop the pods and let their silky, plumed seeds fly to the wind. Their fuzzy stems growing to five feet high contain a whitish liquid, hence the name milkweed. Honeysuckle, meadow rue, field daisies, asters, and blackberries also grow along this section of the walk. We've seen a resident broad-tailed hawk follow the far shoreline in front of a dark pine woodland.

Dave Shepardson, who worked here for many years, designed and engineered the road. About

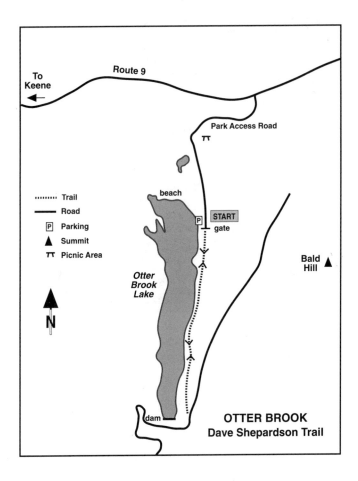

OTTER BROOK
Dave Shepardson Trail

halfway to the dam, the road moves into the trees, rises slightly, descends, then makes a steady climb toward the dam, which was constructed in 1956–1958 as one of sixteen United States Army Corps of Engineers projects to prevent flooding of the Connecticut River basin. Measuring 1,288 feet long, 133 feet high, 700 feet wide at its base, 25 feet wide on top, this dam can hold 17,000 acre-feet of water.

As you walk toward it, the foliage thickens until you're in the woods and the dam is out of sight. In late summer wild grapes hang in green and purple clusters from long, winding, tough brown vines. The marble-size grapes are plentiful.

Red raspberries grow along the road as well as black-eyed Susans, hairy-leafed mullein, and delicate blue chicory flowers. Toward the end of the walk, a wild apple tree and staghorn sumac, with its upright, velvety red flowercones, are visible along the roadside. We've often steeped sumac berries that grow in our yard for a delightful, refreshing drink that tastes like pink lemonade.

Be careful, though, not to mistake poison sumac for staghorn sumac. Poison sumac, with shiny green leaves and white berry clusters that mature in late fall, favors swamp habitats and is poisonous to the touch. Poison sumac doesn't grow on this road but poison ivy does—on the open sections. Poison ivy is a woody vine with three smooth, shiny leaflets, aerial roots, and whitish berrylike fruits, all of which contain urushiol, a skin irritant causing inflammation and watery blisters on contact. If you discover that you've walked

Blackberries, blueberries, and raspberries grow plentifully along sunny roads and trails.

through poison ivy (impossible if you stay on the road), when you get home sponge off your boots and then wash your clothing. In the field, nature has produced a remedy—jewelweed. This small, yellow-orange dainty capped flower nodding on thin, three-foot-high stems may be used as a short-term antidote to alleviate itching. It has worked for us several times for insect bites and allergic reactions. We rub the flower pollen directly on the skin and, amazingly, the itching stops—for a while at any rate.

The trail reaches a cleared area at the top of a hill where an asphalt road provides access to the dam. From the high point on the dam the view of the lake and marsh across to the far end is vast and impressive.

Getting There

From Route 101 in Keene, take Route 10 and 12 north to Route 9 east. Drive about 2 miles up and over two hills to the Otter Brook Recreation Area entrance on the right. Follow the access road down and beside Otter Brook. After crossing a small bridge, drive past the swimming beach to the boat launch ramp and parking area.

Harris Center For Conservation Education
Hancock
7,000-Acre Supersanctuary

Recommended walk: Harriskat Trail,
3 1/2 miles, 2 hours 30 minutes

A gradual climb to the summit of Skatutakee with top-of-the-world views of Hancock village and Grand Monadnock.

Here in the rural southwestern corner of New Hampshire lie brooks, ponds, lakes, woods, hills, and mountains of exceptional repose and beauty. A long vista of these sights, plus a few church steeple tops in valley-nestled villages, awaits you at the end of this stretch-your-legs walk.

Although this trail gradually ascends 660 feet to the 2,000-foot summit, rocks and roots in the path demand extreme caution, a certain agility, and secure footwear. The rewarding views and the wild blueberries at the summit make this a popular trail in summer.

To locate the trailhead, walk on the Harris Center drive to the left of the parking lot after you've picked up a map and brochure about the center's activities (the office is open weekdays, 9:30–5:00).

As an energetic conservation organization the Harris Center teaches environmental literacy to more

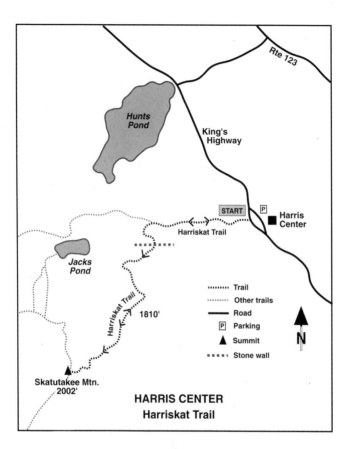

HARRIS CENTER
Harriskat Trail

than 4,000 students in twenty-seven Monadnock-region public and private schools every year, as well as for the general adult communities in the area. Turn right onto King's Highway and walk a few yards down the road to the "Briggs Preserve" sign on your left. Named after King George III in the eighteenth century, King's Highway was used to haul white pines by ox team out of the forest and down to Portsmouth for masts on British tall ships.

Enter the Harriskat Trail on the left. Follow white paint and plastic blazes and an occasional black paw print on boulders at trailside. Watch your step hiking the slope and a moss-covered field of boulders. You'll pass a highland pond surrounded by birch and boulders and walk past a paw print blaze. The birch lend a certain airy lightness to the walk. In early spring and late fall, far below you might be able to spot Jacks

A sample blaze from the Harriskat Trail as it winds its way up Mount Skatutakee.

Pond, which is on the Thumbs Down Trail about 0.5 mile from the Harriskat Trail. Graceful clumps of canoe birch bend and arabesque down the mountainside.

One of the majestic landmarks, about halfway on this trail, is a straight-trunked grand white pine that soars eighty to ninety feet. Keep ascending past the white pine on the right. The rushing water of the brook below and soughing of the wind in the white pines have a similar sound, but if you stop to listen you'll be able to distinguish between them.

Cross a stone wall opening and climb at an easy pace. Traverse another boulder field riddled with the thin trunks of moosewood, also known as striped maple. These green-bark, white-striped trees grow from twenty to thirty feet tall in the eastern mountain ranges and are quite prevalent in New Hampshire. Like all maples, they may be identified by their wing-like seedpods, called samaras.

Harriskat Trail remains green throughout the year. The forest floor is covered with evergreen wood ferns. Their leathery fronds and sturdy two- to three-foot stipes (stems) survive the frost and ice. Bright green moss thrives on the moist granite boulders. Toward the mountaintop, evergreen trees prevail. Silky short-needled fragrant balsam firs keep company with tall white pines and spruce. Some identification tips: white pines have long five-needle bundles while spruce needles are short and grow around the stem; cones hang down from the branches both on white pines and northern species of red, white, and black spruce, but spruce cones usually are rounder and shorter than those of the white pines. Balsam cones grow long, smooth, and upright; their needles have single white lines on the underside. Balsam and pine saplings provide excellent cover for deer and grouse. We encountered several grouse that flew from their roosts deeper into the woods as we approached.

At the "Harris Center" return sign make a sharp right through towering spruce. Wells of sunlight stream through the branches to dapple the pine-needled glade as the trail switches up the slope and along a stone wall.

Soon you come to a wide corridor looking east toward Hancock village with its picturesque white church steeple. The granite ledges below the summit are covered with cherry birch (so called because of its shiny cherry-tree-like bark) and bushy low juniper, an evergreen shrub with bluish needles (one or two juniper berries can pep up a stew and other dishes).

Continue on the trail, passing a paw print rock blaze. The summit is marked by a cairn of piled stones. If it's mid- to late-summer, you may also enjoy the blueberries that abound above tree line on Skatutakee. Take time to enjoy the fantastic view of the surrounding countryside and to identify some of the more prominent peaks.

To the east lies Crotched Mountain, easily recognized by its notched profile. To the south, Grand Monadnock looms large and magnificent; morning is the best time to photograph Grand Monadnock from this perspective. To the north nearby is Bald Mountain and farther north, Lovewell Mountain in the vicinity of Pillsbury State Park.

The trip down a mountain usually turns out to be faster but don't be in too much of a hurry. Haste can lead to strains and sprains. The inverse scenery back to the Harris Center is just as engrossing, and we've found you can discover new sights from a different angle.

The Harris Center Supersanctuary provides school-age children in the area with an outdoor classroom. Weekend field walks, demonstrations, and lectures for both children and adults take place all year long. In the summer the center turns into "Wol's Nest" nature day camp. The center also holds seminars with community conservation groups and planning boards and cooperates with fifteen towns and the New Hampshire legislature to protect the Contoocook River. Hiking the Harriskat Trail can be a good introduction to the center and the beginning of a rewarding environmental relationship.

Getting There

Take Route 123 north from the Hancock Post Office for 2.2 miles. Turn left at the Harris Center sign. Drive 0.5 mile to a pond and a second Harris Center sign. Turn left onto King's Highway, a dirt road. Drive another 0.5 mile or so to the Harris Center. Park for free in the lot at the center.

Pisgah State Park
Chesterfield
13,000 Acres

Recommended walk: Horseshoe
Wildlife Habitat Trail, 1 mile (loop),
1 hour 15 minutes

An identification trail introducing animal and plant habitats at the edge of a wilderness area.

Pisgah State Park is a rugged, forested, wild-feeling backcountry. The upper forest and meadowland northwest of 1,300-foot Mount Pisgah (a biblical term meaning "Gateway to the Promised Land"), once referred to as "Pisgah Wilderness" by locals, attracted early logging operations and water-powered mills. On this walk you'll see a few cellar holes, mill foundations, and other remains of earlier times.

An open meadow presents stunning mountain views from the parking lot. Nearby, the low granite foundation walls of the birthplace of Supreme Court Chief Justice Harlan F. Stone are still standing. The foundation serves as a monument to this extraordinary man. It's also a great place to sit and relax before returning to civilization.

Although this wilderness area is defined as "undeveloped," you'll discover, in fact, that the trails are surprisingly well maintained. The six access roads,

Gateway trailhead into the 13,000-acre Pisgah State Park.

spaced equally around the park, are graded. Signs
indicate parking areas and park gates. The trails are
blazed in different colors and, for the most part, are
well marked. We did talk with a guide from another
park who had been lost in Pisgah on one of the longer,
more isolated trails, but this shorter walk is characteristic of the park and easy to follow.

The key to this trail is the interesting interpretive
overview provided by the park's informative illustrated booklet. It is available at the trailhead in one of two
mailboxes (the other mailbox contains take-home trail
maps) and is to be dropped off at the end of your
walk. Each habitat is numbered and corresponds to
numbered descriptions in the booklet. This trail is
marked with what is supposed to be a turkey track
(although it looked like a tree emblem to us).

The Wildlife Habitat Trail loop includes 16 stations.

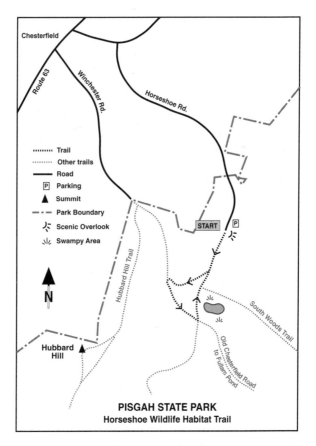

PISGAH STATE PARK
Horseshoe Wildlife Habitat Trail

We've incorporated nine of the stations in our walk, then looped back to the Horseshoe Road parking lot. The full trail is one mile longer. You may certainly walk the whole trail, but we enjoyed this shorter loop.

The wide Horseshoe Trail descends to the right of the parking lot into moist dark woodland. Notice along the banks of the trail where bowling-ball-size chunks of the white quartz prevalent in this section of New Hampshire are embedded. And watch your step. The trail also is a bridle path with frequent messages from horses, especially on the weekends.

Swaying false Solomon's seal border the trail. In spring their white terminal flower clusters hang from curved willow-leafed stems ("real" Solomon's seal produces flowers down the stalk and the berries turn dark blue, not bright red, in the fall). In early spring you'll be accompanied by purple trillium (wake robins) and a profusion of bloodroot. The wide irregular leaf of bloodroot curls tightly around the delicate white petaled bloom, unfurling only when the light reaches the forest floor.

Pass stone steps leading to a well and cistern on your right. After this, the trail forks. Follow the arrow and the turkey track blazes to the right. The first three numbered trail stations draw walkers' attention to meadows and clearings edged by protective cover. These fields and fens bordered by dense juniper and pines, and lower Canada yew, provide temporary lodging and browsing habitats for deer and moose (station 2). Meadows mown in late summer and reclaimed apple trees offer valuable fruit and other food sources for a variety of wildlife.

For a short distance the trail turns grassy. Station 4 indicates a healthy stand of aspen. An aspen grove is an asset in any forested area: For example, one ruffed grouse (sometimes called partridge) depends on the buds of twelve to fourteen full-grown aspen trees to get it through the winter. Woodcocks raise their young in aspen cover, and other forest animals depend on the buds for food as well.

You'll pass a grand old maple tree on the right and continue through a spacious beech and birch forest. In the guide booklet station 5 refers to live trees with hollow cavities ideal for nesting birds, chipmunks, squirrels, and other birds and animals.

A little less than halfway through the loop an arrow on the right of the trail points to the left. Don't go straight. Make a sharp left turn and continue following the turkey track blazes to a turkey roosting site (station 6) in the white pines.

The roosting site is a reminder of the turkey's recent return to this region. Several years ago the New Hampshire Fish and Game Department introduced wild turkeys to the woods of southern New Hampshire. We remember meeting turkey fledglings in the most unlikely places. Confused by their sudden freedom, they wandered aimlessly across roads and one or two gobblers landed in backyards and on town commons. But the vanguard successfully survived the first few arduous winters, and today, turkeys may be included among the ground-dwelling birds of New Hampshire.

At station 7 the walker will observe a beech tree with many beechnut hulls and shells underneath it. Beech, oak, hickory, and other trees with superabundant supplies of nuts and seeds are called "wolf-trees" because of their unusually large, bushy crowns. The crown size is related to unusually high seed production—superproducers of food for deer, turkeys, and other wildlife.

From this point the trail passes between two stone walls. On your right, a partially overgrown marsh area shows the slow transformation by beaver of wetlands to meadow areas (station 8).

The trail narrows to a footpath through marsh grasses and crosses a levee between two small ponds. Walk down the central sand bridge, with water close on either side. Take time to inspect this tannin-colored water habitat at close range. You'll have to negotiate a narrow ditch and mudflat before reaching a junction with a 0.5 mile switchback to the Horseshoe Road parking lot.

A sign on the right a few yards farther points the way to a 1.5-mile side trip to Fullam Pond. The longer interpretive loop also continues in this direction.

The main trail swings back around the tip of the marsh, making a hairpin turn to the left, uphill through a sumac grove. You come out on the Horseshoe Trail in about 0.25 mile. Turn right onto the trail. You'll recognize the old well cistern, which now will be on your left. The parking lot is about another 0.25 mile.

Getting There

On Route 63 drive south into center Chesterfield and turn left onto Horseshoe Road. Follow park signs 1.4 miles to the free parking lot.

Pisgah State Park
Chesterfield
13,000 Acres

Recommended walk: Beal's Knob Trail,
1 mile (loop), 1 hour 15 minutes

---

*A cameo of Pisgah wilderness framing natural scenes from
isolated forests to active beaver ponds.*

This trail evokes a sense of wilderness with long matted grasses and flowers underfoot, ferns swishing against your legs. Long pants and boots are advisable, especially after a rain and against thorny blackberry vines in some sections. Don't let the word "wilderness" deter you. This trail is well marked and offers magical moments from a mountain forest to a beaver pond.

From the parking area cross an open meadow studded with woodpiles, and on the right enter the Beal's Knob Trail at a sign with blue blazes. The variety of wildflowers, if they're in bloom, may slow your progress. On our walk, in the fall, a brilliant parade of goldenrod and asters lighted the way. Cinnamon and other ferns bordered a pathway and tall, thorny stalks of Canada thistle had taken root here and there. The pink, soft, hairlike flowers of these plants produce seeds relished by goldfinches during fall and winter. You may also see wild radish. A far cry from the earth-hugging garden variety, this plant has distinctive

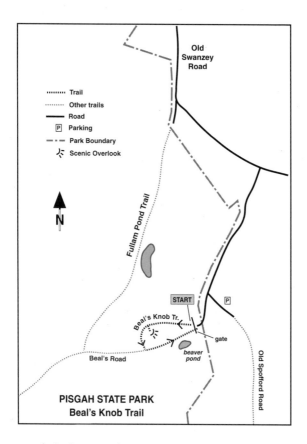

PISGAH STATE PARK
Beal's Knob Trail

ragged dark green leaves spaced widely on a solitary
stalk, often more than five feet tall.

To your right, beyond a toppled stone wall, lies a
new-growth forest of hemlock and goosefoot maple,
so-called because the leaf resembles the foot of a

goose. The goosefoot, also called moosewood or striped maple, also has unique striated green and white smooth bark.

About midway along the trail, turn left on a side trail marked by blue blazes to climb through dense forest upward toward Beal's Knob. Beech trunks, reminiscent of smooth gray elephant legs, show greater, older girth in this upland wood. Follow the blue blazes through black birch and beech trees to the top of Beal's Knob (0.25 mile round-trip from the side-trail junction). On the knob a wide swath of trees has been cut to provide walkers with an excellent tunnel view over the valley toward the mountains in Vermont.

From the summit, backtrack to the main trail. Turn left to continue your walk through an open area of paper birch and goldenrod. A sign nailed to a birch points to "Fullam's Trail" on the right. Turn left onto Beal's Road. Descend slowly with a stone wall on the right. A park entrance sign will be on your left. On your right a large beaver pond will come into full view.

The last time we walked this trail, two beaver were chomping loudly on pondside branches, seemingly oblivious to our whispers. The snap of the camera shutter triggered the warning slap of a beaver tail. Both dived underwater but then resurfaced without much alarm to continue dining. We joined them, having found the biggest, sweetest blackberries within easy reach. Just remember, berries like the same soil as poison ivy, so let your fingers reach for the higher berries.

Continue forward across the other side of the open field and to the park gate.

These wary beaver move away from shore in a pond near Beal's Knob Trail.

We hope this short walk in isolated terrain entices you to discover more of the seven ponds, four highland ridges, and five other trailheads in this undeveloped but well-maintained wildlife preserve.

Getting There

Travel west on Route 9 after Keene. The Chesterfield Gorge Wayside Park is on the right. Exactly 1.5 miles after the gorge, turn left onto Old Chesterfield Road. Make an immediate left onto Tuttle Road and drive less than 0.25 mile to Old Swansey Road. Turn right onto Old Swansey and drive 0.9 mile to a fork. Veer right, staying on Old Swansey Road. (Zinn Road goes to the left.) Drive another 0.9 mile. A small brown Pisgah sign points to the right down a two-rut dirt road. Drive 0.6 mile to a well-marked Pisgah parking area (no fee) near the park gate.

Ashuelot River Park
Keene
44 Acres

Recommended walk: Ashuelot River
Trail, 1 3/4 miles, 45 minutes

A multiuse river trail in the heart of a college town.

The Ashuelot River starts west of Concord, winds
beyond Surry Dam north of Keene, and feeds into the
Connecticut River in the southwest corner of the state.
This urban trail along the river is heavily used. You're
likely to meet a few joggers, biking children, teenagers
taking a shortcut, mothers pushing baby strollers,
senior citizens on riverside benches, and dog walkers.
Nevertheless, this is an enjoyable example of how a
popular in-town trail can create a sense of absorbing
remoteness and connection to the natural world.

The trailhead is located at the far end of a charming small park landscaped by the Old Homestead Garden Club of Keene. Starting at the first cardiovascular
fitness station, follow a worn path along the river
edge.

Continue on the graded pathway. Although you
are on a main trail, overgrown backwaters give this
trail a definite feeling of teeming growth. Vireos war-
ble and flycatchers wag their tails as they perch on
drooping branches over the brown flowing water.

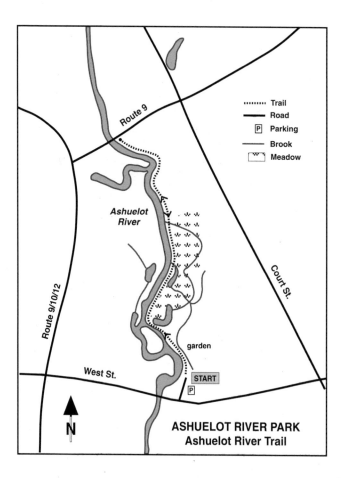

Legend:
- .... Trail
- ▬▬ Road
- P Parking
- —— Brook
- Meadow

Route 9

Route 9/10/12

Ashuelot River

Court St.

garden

West St.

START

P

N

ASHUELOT RIVER PARK
Ashuelot River Trail

The lazy Ashuelot River flows through the city of Keene in an urban park.

Short side paths lead to the riverbank where frogs, turtles, and otters make their homes in the reeds and rushes. Herons use these swampy backwaters as runways. Blue-green darners, the largest and most beautiful dragonflies, alight on arrowheads and pickerel-weed in the sluggish current. They get their unusual name because in the old days they were thought to sew children's mouths closed!

Beneath the waters of the river, a drama is unfolding. Thumb-size dwarf wedge mussels, which survive only in the Ashuelot and Connecticut rivers, are an endangered species. A few years ago, water samples showed toxic amounts of cadmium had leached into the river from new Surry Dam. Although the problem at the dam was resolved and samples today read normal, the wedge mussel population still is endangered. Research is ongoing, but part of the problem may concern the three-inch tessellated darter, which the wedge mussel uses as a host for its larvae.

The Nature Conservancy and New Hampshire Natural Heritage Inventory Program are conducting studies on the darter and on the European zebra mussels, since they've been crowding out native mollusk populations in freshwater lakes and streams across the Northeast. If you peer into the shallows long enough, you may see the mottled, small perchlike darter. But mussels grow primarily in clearer stretches of the gravel river bottom.

When you reach the macadam bike path at Route 9, turn around and backtrack. At midtrail take time to examine a meadow on your left. Shoulder-high weeds, such as milkweed and joe-pye, grow in profusion. (Joe-pye weed's name comes from early legend. The story goes that Joe Pye was a colonial herb doctor who made a successful tonic for diarrhea from the roots of this twelve-foot-high plant. Because of its abundant frosty pink blossoms it also has been dubbed "queen-of-the-meadow.")

During summer, jeweled fritillary butterflies, hummingbirds, and bees feed on the nectar of these meadow flowers. In winter, the taller stalks stick out of snow drifts, and plants like the notorious allergy-producing giant ragweed provide oily seeds for chickadees, titmice, and other year-round birds.

The Ashuelot River Trail is our favorite refuge when we're in Keene. After a busy morning of

A lovely monarch alights along the banks of the Ashuelot.

errands, we enjoy a walk along the peaceful, meandering river followed by a picnic in the lovely ornamental gardens.

Getting There

From Route 101 in Keene, drive north on Route 9/10/12 to West Street, the first exit on the right. Turn right and drive about 0.5 mile. Turn left into Ashuelot River Park set about 100 feet from West Street. Park for free in the parking lot in front of the gardens.

Chesterfield Gorge State Wayside: A Geological Park
Chesterfield
15 Acres

Recommended walk: Gorge Trail,
1 mile (loop), 40 minutes

A graded trail up and down a steep geological rift.

With its heavy snow runoff, spring is the most impressive season to walk above the stream that flows through this narrow rock ravine. The trail loops around paralleling cliffs, crossing two small footbridges. This is a popular, refreshing walk, especially for auto-weary travelers. Pipe railing and wire fencing are posted at sections where the trail comes close to abrupt edges. The walking is safe but keep your eyes open for exposed roots that can be slippery when wet. The barriers don't enhance the natural scene but do provide a measure of safety.

If the visitor center is open, stop in to see historical photographs, antique lumber saws, and other artifacts from the local area.

The trail starts at a sign by the edge of the woods near picnic tables. Follow a wide, 300-yard-long access path down to the first footbridge. Cross the bridge to reach the top of the gorge.

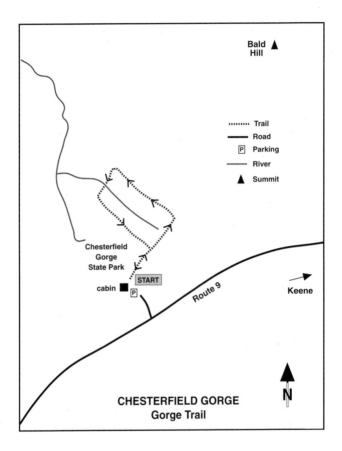

Bald
Hill ▲

.... Trail
▬▬ Road
P Parking
▬▬ River
▲ Summit

Chesterfield
Gorge
State Park

cabin ■   START
P

Route 9

→
Keene

↑
N

CHESTERFIELD GORGE
Gorge Trail

This isn't the Grand Canyon by any means, but compact Chesterfield Gorge gives you an exhilarating walk along its precipitous ledges and edges. The formation of the ancient bedrock foundation at this locality is thought to have begun 460 million years ago, when shallow seas covered this region. As nearby volcanoes erupted, lava and core fragments spewed forth, eventually cooling and hardening into rock. Later, huge boulders were shoved southward by gigantic glacial sheets, scoring the land plates.

Chesterfield Gorge is one of several places around Spofford Lake (about two miles west) where Ammonoosuc block volcanics and white chunks of Clough quartzite are exposed and can easily be seen from the trail.

Two schools of thought describe the origins of the current shape of the gorge. One theory is that the gorge is the result of a basaltic dike, softer than surrounding rock. The basalt eroded away, leaving the dramatic ravine. The second theory proposes that the gorge is not the result of erosion at all but a fault in the earth's crust.

Stepping down the right (east) side of the gorge, you pass by three-flowered wild sarsaparilla (noted for its aromatic root) growing in the leaf duff. Its flowers are arranged in three clusters (the similar ginseng flower cluster grows singly), and its broad leaves grow on horizontal branches from a long stalk. Notice inside the gorge the exuberant birches reaching with their giraffelike necks from the depths of the gorge to the sunlight above. At the bottom of the trail, a second footbridge leads back across the gorge. At this point water echoes down the tight canyon as it tumbles over ledges and boulders, turning into thin sheets of silvery falls.

Groundwater steadily flows down the stream at the bottom of Chesterfield Gorge.

After crossing the bridge, turn left and follow the trail up the other side of the gorge. The climb calls for a slow and steady effort, maybe with a breather now and then to look at the gorge from a different angle.

Getting There

From Keene drive Route 9 west for nearly 6 miles. A road sign indicates the Chesterfield Gorge parking lot on the right. There is no parking fee.

Wantastiquet Natural Area
Hinsdale
847 Acres

Recommended walk: Summit Trail,
$4^1/2$ miles, 2 hours 30 minutes

---

*A vigorous nine-switchback climb to the 1,335-foot summit
overlooking Brattleboro, Vermont, and the Connecticut River.*

The trail to the top of Wantastiquet Mountain is wide
and easy to follow, but the steady uphill angle
requires more effort than a casual stroll. Nine major
switchbacks in the trail wind back and forth up the
mountainside. A small clearing on a rocky ledge at the
top opens up a wonderful, high-level vista. The Connecticut River, the cozy New England town of Brattleboro, Vermont, and the Green Mountains appear to
the west. We found ourselves staring at the mesmerizing scene longer than we do at most trailside vistas.

A green iron pass-through gate plainly marks the
trailhead next to the parking lot (a service road farther
to the left leads alongside the river, but we discovered
far fewer views of the river than we anticipated). The
marker at the parking lot entrance explains that the
rocky road to the summit was built in 1890 for quarry-
ing on the mountain.

No blazes are posted along the trail; none are
needed to keep you on track. Simply follow the wide,

A century-old post marks the road to the summit of Wantastiquet Mountain.

main swath upwards. However, good shoes (not moccasins or sandals) are needed to deal with some sections of loose shale underfoot. Although the incline is steady and easily managed, appropriate shoes also help the descent, when you tend to walk faster and the gravity weight of your body momentum needs secure footing in the sometimes wet and slippery sections.

Grape vines thrive near the trailhead. On the right look for a young sassafras sapling. Rarely seen in New Hampshire, sassafras trees are noted for the irregular shape of their leaves, particularly the mitten-shaped

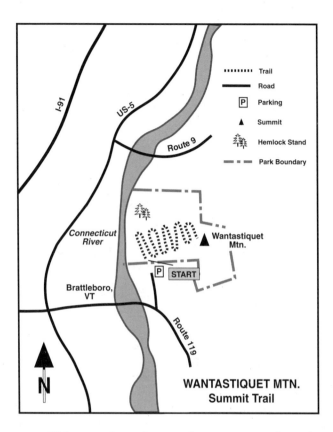

WANTASTIQUET MTN.
Summit Trail

Map legend:
- .... Trail
- —— Road
- P Parking
- ▲ Summit
- 🌲 Hemlock Stand
- –·–·– Park Boundary

I-91 · US-5 · Route 9 · Connecticut River · Wantastiquet Mtn. · Brattleboro, VT · Route 119 · START · N

ones. This was the only sassafras we spotted on the mountain, but it brought memories of seeing many when we hiked the Appalachian Trail in the South.

Soon the trail passes between another iron bar gate (to keep four-wheel vehicles out) and by a large white pine. Ahead on the left two small rock outcroppings give you a chance (and a breather) to see Brattleboro below. These are inviting places to eat lunch or pause if you don't want to go all the way to the summit.

Deep gouges in the trail bear evidence that spring is not the time to walk here. Snow runoff from the mountain comes rushing down and doesn't stick to the washes and the occasional culverts built under the road.

The woods are mixed, but occasionally a solid stand of hemlocks grows trailside. In one section about 0.75 mile up the trail, you'll notice the hemlocks in green and airy contrast to the exposed, slate-colored rock ledge on the right.

The steady ascent slows your pace and gives you pause to notice the wildflowers and plants. Mountain laurel, a relative of the rhododendron, is plentiful in many places; its starlike groups of white and pinkish blooms brighten the woods in late spring and early summer. Lower to the ground, the wraparound leaves of the bloodroot (the name derives from its bright red root and juice) unfold in sunlight to disclose white blossoms on its high spike.

This walk offers rewards both en route and at the summit. You'll notice more rocky ledges as you near the top, particularly on the left. Finally, after what seem to be false signs of the trail's end, the last straight stretch to the summit arrives. Suddenly on the right appears a small clearing with a four-foot granite marker signifying the goal. (The marker is inscribed with: "In memory of Walter H. Childs, erected by his loving friends 1806.")

From this friendly vantage point you can see the subranges of the Green Mountains of Vermont against the far horizon. Below flows the Connecticut River, splicing itself around islands and brushing genteelly past. The whistle of a train may float upward as it moves through town. Past town the concrete ribbon of Interstate 91 stretches north and south. In the distance fields checker the proximate hills with greens and golds against the tessellated greens of the surrounding woods.

Two friends recall lingering at this spot one July afternoon when a red-tailed hawk rode the thermal breeze that rises up the west side of the mountain in warm weather. The hawk was perhaps forty feet away, circling lazily in search of prey; after a few minutes the bird dipped its wing slightly and veered rapidly north, flying along the crest of Wantastiquet.

Return to your starting point via the same path.

Getting There

From Hinsdale drive northwest on Route 119 for about 7 miles. Turn right at the road directly before the steel bridge over the Connecticut River. Drive less than 0.25 mile uphill to the parking area on the right. Two granite posts mark the entrance. From the south side of Brattleboro, Vermont, Main Street, drive over the two sections of the bridge crossing to Route 119. Turn left directly onto the first road after crossing the Connecticut River and go uphill less than 0.25 mile to the parking lot (no fee) on the right. One of the two granite posts reads: "Wantastiquet."

Warner Forest

Walpole

164 Acres

Recommended walk: High Blue Trail,
2 1/2 miles, 45 minutes

---

*An upland walk through hilly fields and woods overlooking
striking views of Grand Monadnock and the Connecticut
River Valley.*

High and hilly, Warner Forest is a remote woodland
with two large, slanting meadows. This indeed is good
deer country. Plenty of deep, cloven hoof marks are
visible in the soft earth. If you do see tracks, a quiet
walk may reward you with a sighting as you crest the
hilltop. A local farmer mows these three meadows for
hay. The nearby protective woods provide shelter for
deer feeding on the grass in these isolated meadows.

First walk from your parked car down the access
road with its stately examples of straight-trunk American beech. Pass a bog on both sides of the dirt road.
Near the bog grow bracken, cinnamon, and interrupted ferns (with their otherwise long, green fronds often
"interrupted" by shriveled up brown pinnae leaf sections). Continue to an aluminum pass-through gate
and Society for the Protection of New Hampshire
Forests (SPNHF or "Forest Society") sign on the left.
The SPNHF received this land from Stephen Warner

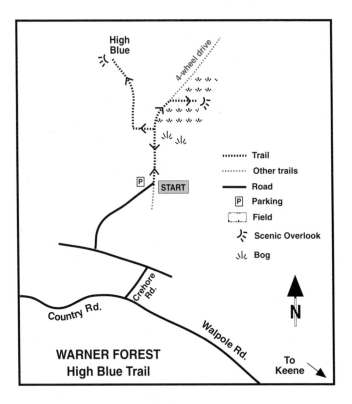

WARNER FOREST
High Blue Trail

in 1981 as a gift for public enjoyment. He called the land "High Blue" for its dramatic upland scenes to the east and west.

At the Forest Society sign, continue straight ahead on the shaded dirt road. (You'll return to this point for the second half of the walk.) Stay on the road as it

The High Blue Trail offers highland meadows where deer feed at dusk.

continues to bend slightly to the right. At a Y junction, proceed to the right (the left fork goes into deep woods) up a sharply graded, short stretch as the road appears to elevate you into the sky. Walk all the way to the top of this rounded, impressive meadow. From the height of land the view sweeps south over portions of Keene in the valley and up to the dominating skyline of Grand Monadnock. You're literally in clover now. And silence. No nearby roads churn up the noise of trucks and cars.

Return downhill backtracking to the Forest Society sign in the woods. Turn right to walk around the pass-through gate and up an overgrown road bordered by woods a short distance to another field.

Continue walking straight uphill along the left edge of the field to the high-left corner of this meadow, where a stone wall and another pass-through gate are located. A trail into the woods begins here. Before proceeding into the woods, be sure to turn around for a long-range view across the field toward pyramidal Grand Monadnock on the far horizon.

A single-lane path ascends easily through lovely, wispy ferns. Soon after passing through the gate and stone wall, look to the left for rocky ledges that mark the characteristic uplifting of the land in this region. A couple minutes later look to the right for remains of a foundation that's been abandoned to the birches and beeches here. The last section of the walk through these thin woods is short and pleasant. A small, dark-water pond twenty feet to the right of the trail lies a few yards before an overlook. On a tree trunk the "High Blue 1,588'" elevation sign marks the spot. Here the view extends from a steep hillside clearing (beginning to grow in) that opens over the Connecticut River valley in the foreground and the Green Mountains of Vermont in the background. This is a refreshing, peaceful spot to spend some time and maybe eat a snack. Return to your car over the same trail, field, and access road.

Getting There

From Keene take Route 12 north to the turnoff to Route 12A. Turn right and drive 0.7 mile to the signal light. Make a sharp left onto Walpole Road and drive 5.9 miles; the road name changes to Old Walpole Road and then to County Road. From a radio antenna in the field on the left, clock 0.9 mile more to Crehore Road.

Turn right on Crehore and drive 0.2 mile. Turn left and drive 0.2 mile more. Turn right onto a dirt road and drive 0.4 mile to a junction with an unimproved road. Park here in mud season and walk 0.3 mile down the road to the Forest Society sign on the left.

From Walpole center, drive south on the main street to County Road, which may not be identified, before going uphill. In 0.5 mile pass Whipple Road on the right. In 6.2 miles turn left on Crehore Road and proceed as above.

Surry Mountain Park
Surry
1,625 Acres

Recommended walk: Beaver Lodge
Trail, 1/2 mile, 30 minutes

A forested walk leading to an active beaver pond and lodge.

Surry Mountain Dam is one of sixteen United States Army Corps of Engineer's dams built for flood control in the Connecticut River basin. The 265-acre lake behind the dam and the surrounding wetlands are home to muskrat, otter, and mink. As the trail name suggests, you may look forward to seeing a beaver lodge, if not the beaver, which often are wary and shy.

Enter the Beaver Lodge Trail at the edge of the woods near a sheltered picnic table area on the southwest corner of the large parking lot. Immediately, the trail leads you up a slight incline through a forest of 80- to 100-foot-high old white pines. The trail crosses the main park entrance road. Walk straight across this road to reconnect with the blazed trail into open mixed woods with three-pronged sarsaparilla plants and young frilly hemlock undergrowth. In the woods, chickadees, pine siskins, and chattering slate-colored catbirds make their presence known. The siskins are the shyest, swooping and flitting about like woodsy goldfinches, only they are fully streaked from head to notched tail.

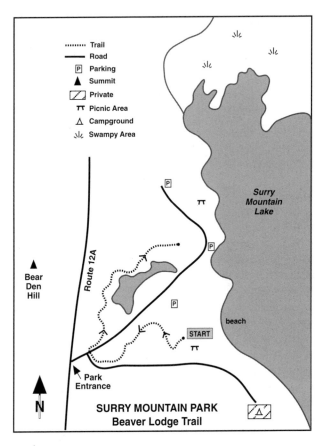

Trail ············
Road ——————
P Parking
▲ Summit
▨ Private
⊤⊤ Picnic Area
△ Campground
⩊ Swampy Area

Surry
Mountain
Lake

Route 12A

▲
Bear
Den
Hill

P

⊤⊤

P

P

beach

START

⊤⊤

↑
Park
Entrance

▲
N

SURRY MOUNTAIN PARK
Beaver Lodge Trail

△

The path is clear, and soon you'll veer left to a handrail leading down a modest incline to a narrow ravine and a swamp edged in spongy peat moss and bracken ferns. Continue across a plywood footbridge.

To the right, water drains over a ledge and down the exposed roots of a yellow birch; walk down a few feet to this pleasant woodland fountain.

Descend along a second ravine. As you approach a marshy pond a short distance farther, step quietly. While we were there, a great blue heron stood in the shallow water imitating one of the gray dead tree stumps. When the prehistoric-looking bird spotted us, it flapped its four-foot wings and circled around to park its four-foot tall body in the rushes. These S-necked waders range from Canada to Mexico and breed in the southern Gulf states.

The beaver lodge is on the far side of the swamp. Beaver are sometimes a nuisance for private landowners, but the mud and branch lodges they build benefit the natural world and wildlife. Their dams provide

A view of the beaver lodge on Beaver Lodge Trail.

flood control, firebreaks, and high water levels during droughts. They also create what naturalists call "edge effects," habitat for deer, woodcock, grouse, and other wildlife that live in semiopen areas.

In the last section of the walk, bracken and sword ferns line the path. Follow the edge of the beaver pond a short distance; the trail is less defined but still faintly visible. Wind through a copse of quaking aspen, which along with the cottonwood is a relative of the poplar family. Poplars are quick-growing trees with heart-shaped or oval leaves that shimmer and dangle in the sunlight. The trembling aspen is a frequent sight in open, sandy areas such as this.

Continue until you come to an overgrown sand road. Turn right and walk through waist-high goldenrod, blackberry bushes, and scrub birch. The walkway emerges onto a mowed lawn behind public rest rooms. Straight ahead, the park road connects with the parking lot and playing field. Note: Since this is a popular recreation area, noise from the swimming beach and the playing field penetrates the woods in the summertime. If you treasure quiet, plan to visit off-season or early in the morning.

Getting There

From Route 101 on the west side of Keene, drive north on Route 12 past Route 9. Turn right at Route 12A. Follow 12A north toward Surry. Go past the sign to Surry Dam and continue about 1 mile to Surry Mountain Lake Recreation Area. Parking is free.

Bear Den Geological Park

Gilsum

60 Acres

Recommended walk: Bear Den Trail,
1 1/4 miles, 1 hour

---

*A treasure trove of geological potholes and rock specimens
in a wild setting.*

The state has suspended active maintenance of this
site and no longer identifies it with a sign, but the area
remains open to the public. Walking into the rocky
woodland leads quickly past exposed bedrock sections
and, later, to unusual natural potholes, the reason it's
called a geological park.

The convoluted terrain of Gilsum holds geological
surprises, and this trail highlights several. Over mil-
lions of years of geological activity, rock plates in the
area pressed and folded over each other, creating
sharp ledges. Water erosion also gouged out potholes
in softer rock.

Begin your walk at the back corner of the parking
lot where a dirt road leads into the woods. Right away
on the left notice a large, energetic hemlock that has
grown out from the fissure of a boulder. A few more
yards to the right and over the first rise in the road, a
sizable vein of white Clough quartzite appears, mixing
with the more prevalent coarse and gray granite, an

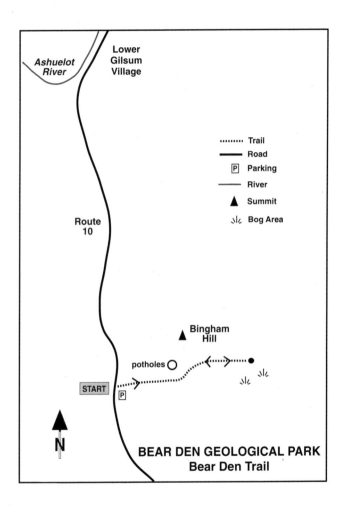

Ashuelot River

Lower Gilsum Village

Route 10

Trail ....
Road ▬▬▬
Parking P
River ▬
Summit ▲
Bog Area ⅃⅃

Bingham Hill

potholes ○

START

P

N

BEAR DEN GEOLOGICAL PARK
Bear Den Trail

Ancient potholes like this one in Bear Den Geological Park evidence the weathering power of water.

example of the geological mixture in this landscape. (Gilsum is widely known for an annual rock hound festival in June—a hard rock fair of the earth, not music—where rock collectors and jewelry makers buy and exchange both what they need and what they can't resist.)

Follow the gentle rise of the road through mixed woods. As you walk Bear Den Trail, you'll see coarse granite in large boulders and outcrops. But many other unseen minerals abound, including beryl, tourmaline, rose quartz, copper, silver, and gold. Strains of pure lead have been found here, and large supplies of mica were once quarried. Garnets were so abundant that early reports of Gilsum refer to streets sparkling dark red after heavy rains, but the washed-out garnets were too small to be useful and valuable.

The trail passes open woods of paper birch, old white pines, and the ever-present American beech. Moosewoods grow along the way. Also called striped maple for its green-with-white striped bark, and goosefoot maple for its broad weblike leaf, the tree is easily spotted, for few young tree trunks are as boldly green as this one.

The trail gets steeper. After about 0.5 mile, the trail crosses a small grassy area at the top of the hill. To the left of this clearing, a granite outcrop protrudes from the hillside. Walk a few yards past the grassy spot as the trail continues downhill. On the left stands an intriguing, two-level concave geological sculpture. This grottolike facade, scraped and smoothed by eons of earth forces, is a captivating sight. On the left of the rock face, a twelve-foot crevice, with natural foot- and handholds, helps you climb to the top of the granite hump to see the potholes on top. These foot-deep, cylindrical holes are fascinating legacies of the profound power of water, which eroded softer rock embedded in the granite. As we did, most likely you'll see water, frogs, and plants in them.

Descend the outcrop and continue on the trail downhill past the grotto and into a secreted pocket of old-growth woods and glacially corrugated earth (a short side path to the left shows the back side of the rock outcrop with its ledges and jumbled boulders). Continue along the main trail to find a primeval scene of bracken ferns, moss-coated hemlocks, white pines,

The "grotto" formation is a popular site at Bear Den Geological Park.

club moss, and other signatures of a moist woodland. Ledges and caves farther back in the woods once were believed to shelter hibernating black bear during the winter. Today, however, the black bear, the predominant species in the region, is only rarely spotted.

Pass a slab bench on the left of the trail and continue walking about fifty yards or so in the woods to the bottom of this wild scene, where grasses and waist-high ferns proliferate along the spongy streambed. This rather open spot makes a good end to the walk, although the trail continues.

Return on the same trail, passing thick, old oaks and hobblebushes with delicate flowers floating like bridal wreaths in the spring. Changing direction also changes the angle of light. Keep an eye out for the sparkle of micaceous rocks, especially as you near the parking lot.

Getting There

From the turnoff to Gilsum center above Keene, drive south on Route 10 for 0.6 mile. Turn left onto a modest-size dirt parking lot. This state site is unmarked.

DePierrefeu-Willard Pond Audubon Wildlife Sanctuary

2,000 Acres
Hancock and Antrim

Recommended walk: Hatch Mill Pond Trail, 1/2 mile (loop), 20 minutes

---

A short, easy loop around a picturesque mill pond.

The Audubon Society of New Hampshire owns thirty-one sanctuaries and preserves totaling 4,300 acres, located in all sections of the state. Willard Pond, as it's known, is one of them. This gentle, isolated pond, with resident loons, is surrounded by woodland, and to the south of it a few hundred yards lies the much smaller Hatch Mill Pond, site of the walk.

Hatch Mill Pond was created when Willard Pond Brook was dammed to support a sawmill. The paper birch, ash, and red maple forest has grown back and some old growth remains. Spruce grouse and chipmunks flutter and chatter in the pine and hemlock undergrowth. You may glimpse resident mallard ducks roosting on the smooth boulders that jut into the marshy pond.

From the parking lot walk left onto a dirt road that leads to Willard Pond and walk a short distance to the

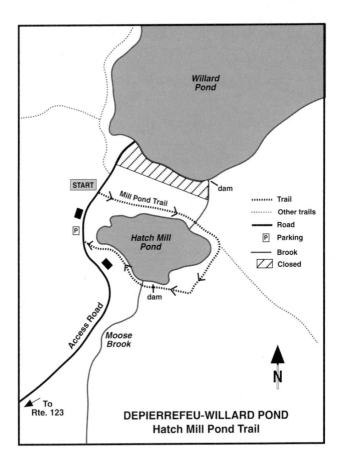

Mill Pond Trail entrance on the right side of the road. (You can see the pond from the road.) Follow yellow metal blazes of the Mill Pond Trail downhill.

In summer the moist inlet, an old dam spill-off from Willard Pond about 0.25 mile to the north, yields bewitching patches of showy cardinal flowers. Crimson flowers glow like torches against the dark water of the meandering stream. These plants are increasingly rare because some less-thoughtful hikers carry them out of the woods. The flowers don't transplant well, however, and survive best in their natural habitat. Please look, but please don't touch.

Cross a wooden bridge over the spillway feeding the pond. Walk into a shadowy white pine and hemlock glade and past a stone wall at the far end of the pond. In fall, ghostly white Indian pipes poke through the pine needle and leaf duff. Deer mushrooms sprout on decaying stumps and logs. Deer may be sighted, especially if you're quiet and walk at dawn and dusk when they like to feed.

Red blazes connect the Mill Pond Trail to the Goodhue Hill Trail entering left. But continue right, following the yellow blazes around the pond past a beaver lodge and across two wooden footbridges over the sawmill dam sluice. Sit awhile on the bridge and listen for the trickle of pond runoff into Moose Brook, the flapping of duck wings, or the chirp of a curious chickadee overhead.

Here the old stone sluice channels Moose Brook runoff, and the trail transits the high foundation of the dam, affording a clear view of Bald Mountain rising above the shore at the Willard Pond swimming beach.

The trail reemerges at the road. Turn right and in a few yards you'll be back at the parking lot.

Water tumbles over the spillway from Willard Pond into Hatch Mill Pond.

In New Hampshire a "pond" may be any body of water ranging in size from a small duck pond such as this one to a 100-acre freshwater tract such as nearby Willard Pond. For this walk, we usually wear swimsuits under our hiking clothes so that afterward we can take a refreshing dip in the clear green water of Willard Pond.

Getting There

From Hancock village drive west 3.7 miles on Route 123 and turn onto an unmarked dirt road to the right. Drive 1.6 miles, bearing left at the fork, to the parking lot for Willard Pond.

Charles L. Peirce Wildlife and Forest Reservation

Stoddard

3,461 Acres

Recommended walk: Tote Road Trail,
1³/₄ miles, 1 hour

A backcountry road over ridges and through deep stands of forested wilderness.

More than ten miles of trails crisscross this large reserve, given to the Society for the Protection of New Hampshire Forests in 1978 by Elizabeth Babcock in honor of local historian and hiker Charles L. Peirce. This walk covers a modest portion of a Forest Society reservation second in size only to the Monadnock Reservation.

The trailhead is plainly marked with a green pass-through bar gate and a large identifying sign. Climbing the first ridge is effortless on a rutted old dirt road; no blazes are used or needed. Right away you walk through a wood of mixed conifers and deciduous trees, with a noticeable scattering of white birch. The hill crests in about 900 feet and then the road turns slightly to the right and slowly descends. A low stone wall parallels the right side of the trail as it moves into more concentrated white pines and American beech.

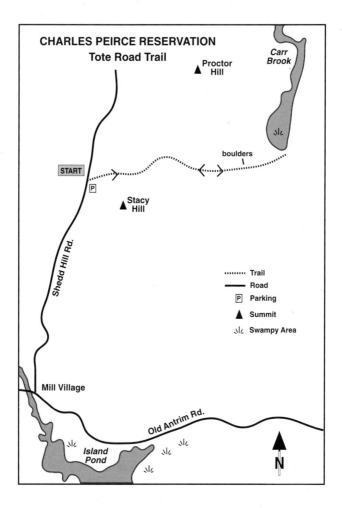

CHARLES PEIRCE RESERVATION
Tote Road Trail

Carr
Brook

▲ Proctor
Hill

boulders

START

P

▲ Stacy
Hill

Shedd Hill Rd.

.... Trail
———— Road
P Parking
▲ Summit
⅄ᵢᵤ Swampy Area

Mill Village

Old Antrim Rd.

Island
Pond

N

Some water runoff crosses under the road in a few spots along here, but unless you're walking after a recent storm the trail is dry all the way.

One time near this section we were strolling along peacefully, about halfway to a bog, when suddenly to the near right the wooded quiet shattered with frantic, deep-sounding thuds. The explosively loud wing beats of a ruffed grouse, no matter how many times we've run across them, ignites our adrenaline and freezes us midstride. Usually, ruffed grouse quickly disappear into the thick summer woods, but in leafless fall you can catch occasional glimpses of their long, black-rimmed, fanlike tails, which distinguish them from the often misidentified—and rarer—spruce grouse, which has shorter, reddish-tinted tail tips. The so-called drumming of the ruffed grouse occurs when the male stands on a fallen log, leans back, and braces himself with his tail feathers. Then he cups his wings and beats them forward and up to make a concussion of the air, causing a "thumping" sound. The faster he beats the more the sound changes into a drumroll that can be heard more than 500 yards away.

Winding down the road, walk a flat section for about 0.25 mile. The trail moves through a section of large, rounded, glacial-age granite boulders in a stand of beech trees.

Just over 0.5 mile into the walk, look on your right for the remnants of a small house. Granite stones are piled in a caved-in twenty-by-fifteen-foot cellar hole. Two large trees and a few saplings grow out of the foundation, testifying to its age. You might still see some old bottles lying in the grassy bottom of the cellar hole, as we did, reminding us of the early glass industry near here. Glassmaking flourished in Stoddard for 30 years beginning in 1842. Choice deposits of clear, fine sand were found in the area and ample firewood was available to generate and sustain the 1,200-degree heat needed to melt the sand. These deposits contained the exact proportion of manganese needed to make the amber and olive green colors that made Stoddard glass famous. Four bottle companies developed and at the height of operation employed 800 blowers, firemen, carry-off boys, woodsmen, and helpers. The factories produced demijohns, snuff bottles, blacking bottles, food jars, rose water bottles, wine bottles, telegraph insulators, and the "Stoddard Stubby," a popular beer bottle of yesteryear. These bottles were shipped by stagecoach through Hancock, Peter-borough, and Milford to Boston and from there throughout the nation.

The trail flattens again a short distance from the cellar hole and soon reaches the bog. This secluded, dark-water marsh is a good, quiet place to rest and snack. Bony, dead tree trunks stand in the water while alder thickets fill in the semicircle background. The road skirts the bog and then heads uphill rather steeply on the other side, continuing to higher ground and Trout Pond, eventually connecting with the five-mile Trout-n-Bacon Trail (named after Trout Pond and Bacon Ledge). However, the bog makes a convenient and interesting terminus for this walk. Return to your car by retracing your route.

A view of the subtle pleasure of the backcountry in the fall.

Getting There

From Route 9 in Stoddard, turn onto Route 123 north. In 0.9 mile pass Island Pond on the right. Continue to a crossroad with a fire station on the right-hand corner. Turn right, cross a small bridge, and turn left (Shedd Hill Road). Ascend 0.5 mile, up a steep hill. At the top of the hill, park on the roadside at the sign "Society for the Protection of New Hampshire Forests."

McCabe Forest Wildlife Demonstration Woodlot
Antrim
192 Acres

Recommended walk: McCabe Forest Trail,
$1^1/_2$ miles (loop), 1 hour 30 minutes

A diverse, 18-station trail through meadows and forests along the dark, meandering Contoocook River.

For many years Dorothy McCabe listened to suggestions of how to use the land she and her husband, John, bought and improved since 1943. Developers plied her with schemes of turning the old fallow farm fields, forests, and river edge into a golf course, house lots with river views, an office building complex, or a racetrack. In 1982 she instead deeded her land and home to the Society for the Protection of New Hampshire Forests to manage for education, wildlife, and forest products. What a wonderful decision.

Today this is one of five demonstration wildlife habitat areas in the state, each with its own guidebook, and offers a showcase for home owners interested in making private properties more attractive to wildlife. For this site well-known naturalist Ted Levin (with help on the wildlife management text) wrote "Changing Hands, Changing Lands," an informative booklet,

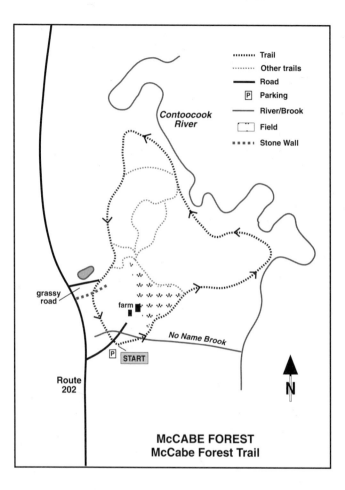

Trail
Other trails
Road
P Parking
River/Brook
Field
Stone Wall

Contoocook River

grassy road

farm

P
START

No Name Brook

Route 202

N

**McCABE FOREST
McCabe Forest Trail**

artistically illustrated by Joan Waltermire. These handsome guides, left in the mailbox beside the kiosk, are sometimes taken as keepsakes and thus are in short supply; they should be returned at the end of your walk. However, this trail is well marked and easy to follow. We enjoy McCabe most in early spring or late fall; during summer the Contoocook River disappears from view in a jungle of weeds, trees, and bushes.

Small white arrows on a dark green background indicate various trail sights and habitats. Follow these arrows and beige blazes behind the kiosk and down an embankment past Ice Age boulders deposited here 12,000 years ago. Cross No Name Brook using stepping stones. Nearby, groundwater "seeps" push to the surface, providing drinking holes for raccoon, skunk, mink, weasels, wild turkey, and other wildlife during the winter when the brook and river are iced over (this is explained at station 2 in the guidebook).

Walk across an old brickyard (station 3). John Hopkins worked a farm here and also fabricated bricks for more than fifty years, using the clay and glacial sand deposits on his property.

In the 1800s, the Contoocook River valley was a fertile farming area with extensive meadows and grasslands (station 4) for sheep and cattle grazing. "Successional communities" have since taken over and reclaimed the land. This term crops up often in woodlot management. Succession means that one species or community of plants gives way to another. For instance, mowed meadows, when left fallow, give way to perennial weeds such as aster, fleabane, and milkweed. Berries and shrubs, whose seeds are dispersed by birds living in and near open fields, soon crowd out the weeds. Eventually, smaller, sun-loving trees like gray aspens, chokecherries, and sumac take over. Next in succession come the tall shade trees—white pine, hemlock, beech, birch, and oaks.

In McCabe Forest, twenty old apple trees have been freed from competing shade trees and revitalized by judicious pruning. This practice, called "tree release," helps to attract wildlife. Many times we've come across deer, porcupine, squirrels, raccoon, and other animals eating apples and crab apples from trees like these.

At a double blaze continue straight ahead. The "Main Trail" sign is clearly placed. About 100 yards beyond, look for an aspen grove to the left (station 5). In lively prose, the booklet describes aspens as "a smorgasbord of leaves, stems, branches, buds, flowers, seeds, roots and rootlets, sap, and bark that are gnawed, chewed, bitten, nipped, swallowed, shredded, rolled, drained, skeletonized, perforated, peeled, masticated, and sucked dry by animals from moose to mites." Author Ted Levin cites as an example that one ruffed grouse will eat the buds from twelve to fourteen aspens during a winter.

Walk about 100 feet to reach a stone wall on your right (station 6). The eastern milk snake lives in the crevices of stone walls like the ones on this property. The milk snake resembles the large three- to four-foot copper-colored mottled copperhead, also known in the South as the water moccasin, but it is not poisonous.

The eastern milk snake rarely bites. Leave it alone and it will go about the business of keeping the mole, vole, mouse, rat, and chipmunk rodent population in check.

During the summer, when snakes aren't hibernating in underground burrows or beneath rocks, they are more likely to be found in ponds or on lakeshores than on a forest trail like McCabe. The water is warmer and granite boulders along ponds make good sunning spots. Tadpoles, salamanders, and frogs are in abundant supply and attract summering reptiles.

Turn right and walk adjacent the stone wall to the bank of the Contoocook River (station 7), a short jog from the trail. Take time to watch the lazy, tannin-colored Contoocook River flow north where it disem-

The north-flowing Contoocook River was once the home territory of the Pennacook tribe.

bogues at the Merrimack River above Concord. You are following the path of the Pennacook Indians who tilled the rich soil of the floodplain to grow squash, beans, and corn long before European settlers arrived here in the mid-eighteenth century. The Contoocook Trail (now U.S. 202 from Jaffrey to Concord) once connected many small Pennacook villages along the river.

At a pair of blazes walk ahead a few yards on a side path to the riverbank (station 8). In spring and summer painted turtles bask in the sun on fallen river logs. Golden perch and pickerel lay chainlike egg masses by the thousands. Quiet backwaters support bottom-feeding bass. Green, blue, and white herons ply the river as a flyway for daily fishing expeditions.

Meanders and oxbows (described at station 9 of the booklet) are river-related terms. The river "meanders," or winds in and out, turning and snaking over the land. The older the river, the more meanders and S curves it acquires. An oxbow is a U-shaped lake or pond that takes its name from its similarity to an ox yoke. When river sediment closes off the ends of a river meander, an oxbow lake forms. An oxbow lake eventually fills in with alluvium left by receding spring floods (station 11 is an example of a filled-in oxbow). Successional plant communities press in, slowly reclaiming the land.

The trail veers slightly away from the river as you cross a footbridge and walk past towering white pines (station 12). Two trails enter from the left, but you stay right. Make sure to keep the river channel in eyeshot on your right and the beige blazes in view as you walk

Eastern white pine cones have a distinctive shape and size.

straight ahead through a deeryard in a hemlock grove (station 13).

A little farther on, turn left away from the river and through a spacious oak grove. Here's another example of how to encourage wildlife: The oaks (station 14) have been thinned and "released" so that the crowns of the trees are allowed to branch out and produce more acorns. The "released" oaks provide abundant food for birds and animals. Here you may see squirrels and even blue jays storing acorns. Jays, as it happens, are excellent reforesters. Four dozen jays, Levin points out, can hide about 150,000 acorns in one month. They often bury the acorns just beneath the leaf mulch, which leads to a much higher germination rate than occurs when the nuts naturally fall from the tree. Thus, these squawking, perky, blue-hooded birds help maintain the oak forest that sustains them.

At a double blaze, loop to the left and follow beige blazes onto a wide, roadlike trail. Swerve around to a stand of sun-loving gray birch (station 15). In a successional community, shade trees like these establish the final stage of reclamation.

In spring, vernal pools of rainwater and snowmelt fill declivities on the forest floor. Station 16 shows one of these pools, about 15 feet in diameter, located about 25 feet off the trail to the left. Animals prefer to drink running brook water. However, these pools have an additional purpose. They are home to tree frogs (peepers), whose "froggy-went-a-courtin'" chorus reaches a shrill crescendo on warm New Hampshire evenings. Frogs, salamanders, and other amphibians prefer these quiet pools for breeding and spawning because predatory egg-and-tadpole-eating fish are absent.

Continue on the main trail veering to the right as connecting trails join it from the left. A small clearing on the right illustrates the conditions for developing biodiversity (a variety of species). First to seed are the yellow birch sprouts, then the spinning propeller-type wings of the maple seedpods, and finally the heavy beechnuts. Light wells created by toppled forest trees soon refill with seedlings of these species.

Continue to veer right and climb to a meadow on your left. Pass through an opening in the stone wall at the corner of a berry-filled field (station 17). Purple finches (New Hampshire's state bird), bluebirds, catbirds, robins, and other birds delight in the abundance of raspberries, blueberries, elderberries, blackberries, and sumac fruit found in meadows like this. Birds also disperse the seeds to other open areas, thus ensuring a plentiful diet the following summer.

Climb up a grassy knoll. At the arrow and yellow blaze on a trunk, turn right. (Note: The farmhouse and barn are private property.) Pass through another opening in another stone wall to enter a grassy area with a small pond on the right. This meadow, once a staging field for a logging operation, has been graded, fertilized, and replanted with grass and clover to attract wild turkey and other wildlife.

U.S. 202 lies directly ahead; if you wish, you may walk the road back to your car. Otherwise, turn left at the pond and follow yellow blazes to return to the parking area. The remaining 0.2 mile of the trail covers rocky terrain. Watch your step heading into a dry rocky creek bed and through the mixed hardwood forest (station 18). The blazes come out directly across from the McCabe Forest parking entrance.

Getting There

From Antrim drive north and at the junction of Route 31 and U.S. 202 in the town center, take U.S. 202 to the right for 0.2 mile to Elm Street. Turn right onto Elm Street and drive 0.1 mile to the "Trail Parking" sign on your right.

Fox State Forest
Hillsborough
1,445 Acres

Recommended walk: Tree Identification
Trail, 1/2 mile (loop), 30 minutes

A short jaunt on a hillside with a variety of hardwoods and softwoods.

Over the years, generous people who loved the New Hampshire woods have donated their land to the state for use by the general public. One of these donors was Bostonian Caroline A. Fox, who summered here. She gave her house and 348 surrounding acres to New Hampshire in 1922. Bordering acreage and improvements were later added, including, in 1972, an environmental center near the park office. This site also serves as headquarters for the southern region of the Division of Forests and Lands.

We found that spending a brief time on Fox Forest's Tree Identification Trail helped us to enjoy some of the other twenty miles of footpaths in Fox Forest. Large, clear, informative signs placed in front of certain trees line this loop trail as it runs through the edge of the woods near the parking lot.

More than 86 percent of New Hampshire land is forested, the highest percentage for a state in the nation after Maine. About 14 percent of that land is owned by

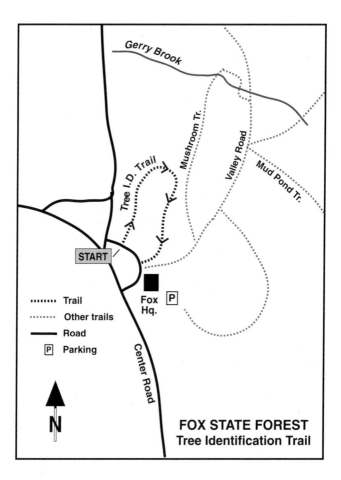

FOX STATE FOREST
Tree Identification Trail

An airy canopy along the Tree Identification Trail in Fox State Forest.

state and national agencies, the rest by private interests. Seventy-four species of trees (62 hardwoods, 12 softwoods) are native to the state. The most common of these are identified on this informative trail.

Begin beyond the end of the asphalt parking lot; signs direct you to the entrance of the "Tree ID" trail. Look for white blazes painted on tree trunks.

As you begin the trail, the tall, straight red (Norway) pines are easily identified by long two- and three-needle clusters and the reddish underbark of their deep, scaly exteriors. Ahead on the right you'll notice the family resemblance between two other trees, poplars and quaking aspens. The leaves of both trees have long stems that allow the leaves to flutter in the slightest breeze.

The trail eases down a hillside. On the right a marker points out a balsam fir, one of the more popular Christmas trees when cut young. Young or old, the balsam fir is recognized by its densely needled branches and tight upright cones. It grows with a symmetrical silhouette. Boy and Girl Scouts once were taught that balsam branches make good outdoor sleeping "mattresses" because of their soft, flat, springy, close-knit branches. Now, however, such reckless cutting is discouraged. These firs also are known for their round extrusions of balsam sap, the fragrant resin so familiar at Christmastime.

Farther ahead on the right a sign identifies an American basswood (also known by its other, lilting name, the linden tree). This full-leafed, bulky tree casts lots of shade as it grows sometimes to heights of 100 feet. Its rounded, heart-shaped leaf (with one lobe raised slightly higher than the other to offset an otherwise perfect symmetry) is the tree's most identifiable feature.

Deeper down the hillside, a hop hornbeam (also known as ironwood because of its extraordinarily hard, tough wood) grows on the left. This relatively short tree, with corrugated brown bark, is named for the catkinlike hop fruits that hang from beech-looking leaves. The American hornbeam, shorter than the hop hornbeam, is also known as blue beech for its bluish gray bark.

About a third of the way on the trail, a Douglas fir grows on the left. Little seen in the East, the Douglas fir is actually a relative of the hemlock. While hemlocks are among the longest living trees, Douglas firs are the tallest, sometimes extending 200 feet. Their short needles spiraling around the branch and the "threads" extending from their cones give the tree a wispy appearance.

Cross a stone wall and bear right through the woods. A few yards farther, next to the trail on the left, grows a striking black birch. The birch family is so frequently associated with the white and paper birches that a black birch seems a contradiction in terms. But notice the short, horizontal, pencillike markings on the bark found in all birches. The leaf shapes differ, however. Gray (also known as silver) birch leaves are clearly triangular with long, pointed tips while paper and black birch leaves are more oval.

This trail gives you a chance to learn some of the different trees within major, familiar species, such as the oaks and maples scattered about. Northern red oak, for instance, grows long, fattish leaves with only a few teeth, while the white oak sports deep lobes and no teeth. The red maple has three basic, simple lobes with virtually no tooth ornamentation while the silver maple grows long, well-delineated lobes with many pointed teeth.

Ahead, on the right, a white ash is identified. Young ashes can be recognized for their tall, thin, grayish trunks without low-lying branches. Their compound oval leaves grow usually in clusters of seven, all about the same size—six opposite pairs along the stem, one at the tip of the cluster.

The last tree identified is a paper birch with its typical snow-white bark that peels away from the trunk like an ancient Greek scroll (don't peel it yourself, of course—you could damage the tree). The trail then moves into the open, between tall woods on the left and tall meadow scrub growth on the right. Continue to the T junction with other trails, turn right, and walk the short distance uphill to the parking lot.

Getting There

From the center of Hillsborough, drive north on Route 149 about 3 miles. The entrance and office to Fox Forest are clearly marked on the right.

Fox State Forest
Hillsborough
1,445 Acres

Recommended walk: Mushroom Trail,
1 mile (loop), 1 hour

An adventuresome mushroom-hunting trail through a forest of conifers.

The Mushroom Trail meanders in a loop through part of the 20-acre Hemlock Ravine down to Gerry Brook and back up Valley Road. Mushrooms burst through the deep hemlock needle carpet, especially in summer and fall. Some mushrooms grow in the vicinity of certain trees and plants and actually are connected by underground strands to tree rootlets in an extensive network. A symbiotic mushroom-tree arrangement is known as *mycorrhiza*. This particular forest produces saucer-size, cream-colored lactarius mushrooms and huge boletes that look like overturned bowls. A mushroom identification book is a definite asset. This trail has mushroom-shaped white blazes, and the beginning of the trailhead is labeled with a sign on the left of Valley Road (a dirt forest service access road) at the left of the office.

Follow the trail through a stand of white pine. In fall, long pine cone husks often litter areas around the dark trunks. Red and gray squirrels and chipmunks

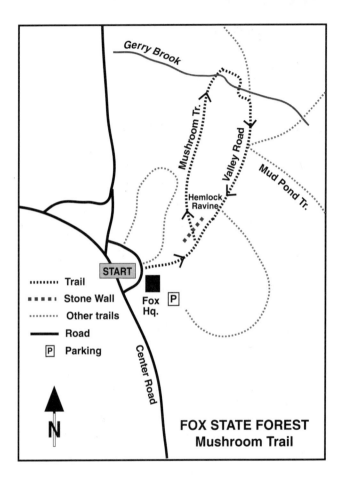

Gerry Brook

Mushroom Tr.

Valley Road

Mud Pond Tr.

Hemlock
Ravine

START

Fox
Hq.

P

.... Trail
▪▪▪▪ Stone Wall
.... Other trails
—— Road
P Parking

N

Center Road

FOX STATE FOREST
Mushroom Trail

This huge bolete is just one of the many samples to be found along the Fox State Forest Mushroom Trail.

relish the pine seeds hidden along the central cone, leaving piles of wooden cone-petals on the forest floor.

A dramatic spill of glacial erratic boulders in the spacious woods gives shade to patches of spleenwort, delicate wood ferns, and waist-high interrupted ferns. (The fronds of some of these ferns are interrupted by hanging brown fertile seed sacks at midstem.)

Follow the trail downhill to the right. The mushroom blazes are difficult to spot here. Veer left and pass through an opening in a stone wall. With more giant boulders on your left, enter Hemlock Ravine, one of the oldest stands of trees in Fox Forest. Hemlocks like this serve as deeryards in winter. Their spreading limbs keep winter snows from accumulating on the ground and provide deer shelter from gale winds and winter storms.

Hemlock Ravine seems open, but the forest floor is littered with broken limbs and fallen trunks. You have to negotiate a few that block the trail; you may also ponder over blazes a bit. Keep descending steadily past a few white birch and tall hemlocks. Gerry Brook winds through the ravine. You'll cross the brook and immediately turn right onto Valley Road. Near the brook, mushrooms cluster at the base of tree trunks and around rocks. One day we discovered a thick-stemmed king bolete eight inches in diameter, looking like a leathery rust-colored helmet.

A second loop of the Mushroom Trail comes in about a third of a mile on the left of Valley Road. However, we found this loop required bushwhacking through a tangle of briars and weeds. This really isn't good mushroom habitat anyway, so we recommend only the first Mushroom Trail loop. At the top of the hill, on your right, you'll recognize the overgrown field you first walked along and the stately row of pines and spruce leading back to the paved road and parking lot.

Getting There

From the center of Hillsborough, drive north on Route 149 about 3 miles. The entrance and office to Fox Forest are clearly marked on the right.

Fox State Forest
Hillsborough
1,445 Acres

Recommended walk: Mud Pond Trail,
3¹/₄ miles, 2 hours

---

*After winding through a virgin white pine forest, the trail
leads to a kettle hole pond.*

The Mud Pond Trail winds through sky-high mixed
woods, across an ever-running brook, alongside a
marsh thicket, uphill slightly through more open
woods, and then down to intriguing Mud Pond. The
walk keeps you away from town sights and sounds
long enough to feel the isolation of this old forest.

As with the Mushroom Trail, this one begins on
the same access road to the left of the office. A sign
points the way downhill to the right of a meadow
overgrown with black-eyed Susans, purple asters,
highbush blueberries, tall, spiky wild radish, and
other plants that favor the sunlight. At the bottom of
the meadow go straight to the "Tree ID" sign on the
left and descend steadily into the woods.

Follow the vertical, oblong white blazes, bisected
by a red stripe, that are painted on trees along the trail.

Proceed downhill past turnoffs to the Mushroom
Trail. Near the right turnoff, notice how forest management by tree thinning allows vital sunlight to

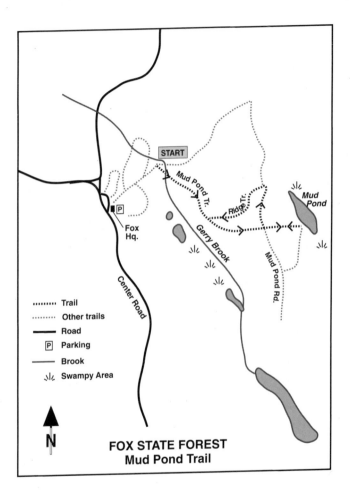

START

Mud Pond Tr.

Ridge Tr.

Mud
Pond

Gerry Brook

Mud Pond Rd.

Fox
Hq.

P

Center Road

- ········· Trail
- ········· Other trails
- ▬▬ Road
- P Parking
- ── Brook
- ⸜⊾ Swampy Area

N

FOX STATE FOREST
Mud Pond Trail

stream down to the forest floor. This nourishes trees to grow their crowns bigger and thicker. It also encourages flowering plants and ground covers. As a result, the overall forest becomes healthier and, if designed for harvesting timber, produces straighter trunks and fewer diseased trees.

As you approach the forest bottomland, the Mud Pond Trail (joining with the Ridge Trail for a stretch) turns left. Near this turn notice the spidery roots of a large yellow birch that have entwined a boulder to the right of the trail.

After crossing a footbridge over Gerry Brook, follow a Mud Pond Trail arrow to the right and continue following the white oblong blazes with the red stripe. Here the trail passes very thick, tall white pines, among the longest-lived trees in New Hampshire. In pre-Revolutionary years the best white pines were reserved for the British navy, who used them for ship masts. This section grows thicker, more crowded, less manicured. Less sunlight now filters to the forest floor; together with a nearby marsh that keeps moisture present, this results in more shade-thriving moss on exposed stone, boulders, and tree trunks.

The trail narrows along an overgrown drainage marsh of Gerry Brook and opens up as you continue past an ancient stone wall. Wind through a few chunky boulders before the trail opens up again, and soon you come to a T junction. A sign for Mud Pond points you to the right and then almost immediately to a left turn as you now follow white dot blazes.

The trail covers high, dry ground and if something minuscule leaps out of your way, it's probably a tree frog. The size of a thumb, sometimes smaller, these midget members of the tree toad family live in the woods and near water. The most seen of New Hampshire's twenty-five species are the green and gray tree frogs and the spring peepers. They can change color; the half dozen we saw were camouflaged to match the brown leaves and needles underfoot. They're a challenge to see even after you spot them jumping away. In spring you can hear the male peepers near ponds calling for mates. When groups of males get together and shout out their high-pitched peeps, they make an interesting chorus.

The trail moves through more open woods again, with a marshy thicket on the right. Continue straight ahead past a blue-dot trail that enters on the right. Don't let this connector tempt you; despite the open appearance, the trail doesn't lead to the pond. Continue straight, climbing slightly to higher ground. A short distance ahead, one mile from the trailhead, a dirt road (Mud Pond Road) crosses the trail. A sign points the way to "Mud Pond Boardwalk."

Across the road and into the beech trees the trail descends toward Mud Pond and its surrounding bog. Blue jays will no doubt screech warnings of your presence as they did for us. Glimmers of blue water show through the woods as you approach the pond. Tread softly and you might catch glimpses of ducks before they see and hear you.

This glacial kettle hole can be seen on the Mud Pond Trail.

Mud Pond Bog is a kettle hole perhaps 20,000 years old. Evidently, when glaciers retreated during the last major Ice Age, a huge block of ice formed a sink that eventually held the melt-off and created this pond. A boardwalk supports you along the pond edge where a mix of swamp alder, asters, and pontoonlike clumps of sphagnum moss grow. The solid boardwalk turns into single logs laid directly on the floating, bouncy moss. It's something like a trampoline walk. Go as far as the gelatinlike shoreline challenges your good judgment.

To return to the trailhead, backtrack the board-walk and the trail to Mud Pond Road less than 0.5 mile away. At the road turn right (this adds about a mile of different terrain so you won't have to back-track the entire trail). Follow this easy-walking, shaded road until you see the Ridge Trail connection on the left, about 0.5 mile from Mud Pond. Be on the lookout because the trail opening is not easily noticeable (the trail sign faces walkers approaching from the other direction). Turn left and again follow white blazes with the red stripe in the center. Descend through comfortable, mixed woods. Soon the trail parallels a brook on the right until you cross it ahead. The trail returns to the T junction where the Ridge Trail meets the Mud Pond Trail. Follow the sign "To Fox HDQTS" to the right; you're now back in familiar territory as you eventually cross the footbridge over Gerry Brook and head up the long hill to the trailhead.

Getting There

From the center of Hillsborough, drive north on Route 149 about 3 miles. The entrance and office to Fox State Forest are clearly marked on the right.

Pillsbury State Park
Washington
8,110 Acres

Recommended walk: North Pond Trail,
1 mile, 45 minutes

A north country lake and spectacular open campsite provide a striking setting.

This short trail is a gem. North Pond affords a good chance for sighting beaver activity and possibly even a moose or black bear. This walk takes you from Pillsbury State Park's picnic area along Mill Pond, then up to North Pond. Most of the route follows a dirt logging road. One note of caution: Logging operations have taken place here in the past, especially between Labor Day and Memorial Day. Heavy equipment may maneuver down the rutted logging roads that hikers use to reach various trails in the park.

Start at the road beyond the picnic tables and through an orange bar gate. Mill Pond, on the right, will scarcely be visible in summer, but it sparkles through young forest on late fall days.

At double-blue blazes on the right of the dirt road, turn left onto the trail marked by a "North Pond-Clemac Trail" sign. Walk about .25 mile through mixed hardwoods and heart-leafed hobblebush. In a backwater to your right you'll pass a neatly construct-

This idyllic campsite lies in the wilderness area of Pillsbury State Park.

ed beaver lodge. Beyond the lodge, on the right, the woods suddenly open onto a grassy area with a spectacular shore view across clear bright North Pond to distant Bryant Mountain (2,260 feet). This is a designated wilderness campsite. Weekdays and off-season it's unlikely to be occupied. Walk around to your right and examine the mud-branch dam and musical trickling spillway. Beaver cut fresh twigs and store them at the base of the lodge to provide food through the long New England winter.

On the off-chance that this lovely spot has been taken, respect the camper's privacy and continue a few yards farther on the Clemac Trail. Find an opening in the vegetation on the shore of North Pond and walk a

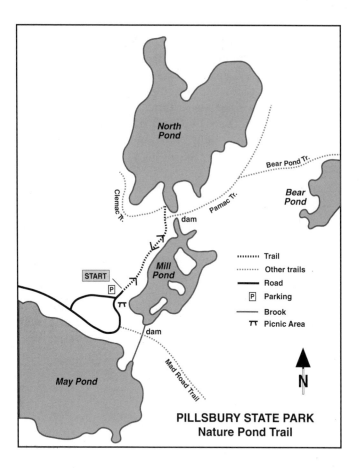

North
Pond

Bear Pond Tr.

Clemac Tr.

Pamac Tr.

Bear
Pond

dam

Mill
Pond

START

P

TT

Trail
Other trails
Road
Parking
Brook
Picnic Area

dam

Mad Road Trail

May Pond

N

PILLSBURY STATE PARK
Nature Pond Trail

few feet down to admire the clear water and sheer isolation of this wild north country lake.

Clemac Trail loops a mile farther past the pond to a landmark called Balance Rock and back to the paved access road if you wish to continue your walk. But for us, any more seemed superfluous. The culmination at this grassy idyllic spot by North Pond imprints on the memory and lingers long after you've reversed direction and headed back to your car near the picnic area.

Getting There

From Route 31, 9 miles south of Newport and 1.5 miles north of Washington, turn into the Pillsbury State Park entrance. Take the park access road 1 mile to a picnic area overlooking the end of Mill Pond. Turn to the left of the lake on a dirt park road, passing more picnic tables under some large maples. A weathered sign, "5-Summers/Monadnock-Sunapee Trail," is tacked on a tree to the left near a table. Park here. Enter the logging road behind an orange gate with a sign: "This Road Not Maintained."

Pillsbury State Park
Washington
8,110 Acres

Recommended walk: Mad Road Trail
to Bacon Pond, 2 miles, 1 hour

A flat woodland road leading to a peaceful, isolated pond.

The pleasure of this walk is more from the journey than the destination. Ninety percent of the trail covers level terrain, through young mixed woods and into the silence of backcountry.

One mile from Pillsbury State Park's entrance on the main access road, look to the right for a gray utility barn. Park at the barn or nearby. On the barn's wall is a large, engraved map of the area. To the left of the barn, you'll see a sign on your right reading "Bridge Ahead" as you walk downhill a little. The bridge leads you past a picturesque, craggy-rock dam site where water runoff flows from Mill Pond into May Pond, falling 36 feet in an eighth of a mile.

After crossing the bridge, veer to the right heading uphill to old Mad Road. This road was once used to haul timber to the water-powered sawmill. Follow the grassy, two-rutted road for the entire walk; no blazes are necessary, although you'll see yellow markers for snowmobile routes in this section of the park.

The woods are airy and open in many places, which

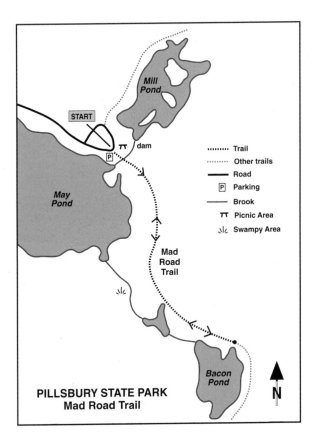

Trail
Other trails
Road
P Parking
Brook
TT Picnic Area
⊻ Swampy Area

Mill Pond

START

TT dam

P

May Pond

Mad Road Trail

⊻

Bacon Pond

N

PILLSBURY STATE PARK
Mad Road Trail

means in late summer you'll likely see clumps of gold-enrod and the ubiquitous pink or purple asters so prevalent in New Hampshire; their small, narrow-petaled, daisylike flowers bloom on long stalks in late summer.

At the beginning of the trail, where it's especially moist, some goosefoot maple saplings, with characteristic toothed, three-tipped leaves, are easily spotted. We saw good examples of interrupted ferns (interrupted by brown, shriveled seed sacs midway up the stalk) and cinnamon ferns (similar in form but not "interrupted").

Since this is a regenerated lumber-cutting area, the woods are well populated with opportunistic trees—aspens, birches, pines. Look for good examples of quaking aspens with their nearly circular leaves shaking and quaking at the slightest breeze because of the extralong stems. (Another identification mark of the quaking aspen is the flattened leafstalk.) Its cousin the large-tooth aspen is similar, but the sturdier leaf displays fewer and longer teeth.

At about 0.75 mile into the walk and on the right through the trees, you'll catch glimpses of the swamplike outlet of Bacon Pond into May Pond. Look on the left of the trail around here for white ash saplings. Usually slightly darker gray than beech, young white ash are widespread in the region and grow straight, narrow, and high before branching out. Their long, oval leaves grow seven to a cluster—three pairs with each pair of stems directly opposite each other, and the seventh leaf at the tip of the cluster.

Up ahead, a small water culvert crosses under the road to the pond. About 80 yards from the culvert is an unmarked, hard-to-see access trail on the right leading to the pond. The junction is at two big maple trees. Take this short side trail only if you're wearing water-resistant shoes or boots or don't mind getting your feet wet. Follow the faint trail through some rocky stretches and, closer to the ponds spongy terrain. Weedy along much of its shore, isolated Bacon Pond is a prime possibility for spotting moose increasingly seen in this area and throughout New Hampshire. The great, gangly animals like to feed on wetland plants.

Large patches of golden thread, a ground cover of sturdy, dark green leaves with white lines down the centers, lend the scene a carpeted richness. You may not find places to sit along the shoreline, but the pond has a keen, pleasant sense of isolation.

Once back on the main trail, return over the same route to your car. On the other hand, if you want to continue down Mad Road Trail, you'll curve to the right halfway around Bacon Pond. About 0.25 mile from this point a connecting trail on the left leads you 0.3 mile to meet the 52-mile Monadnock-Sunapee Trail, a footpath linking the summits of Grand Monadnock and Mount Sunapee.

Getting There

From Route 31, 9 miles south of Newport and 1.5 miles north of Washington, turn into the entrance to Pillsbury State Park. Drive 1 mile past the park office, Butterfield and May ponds, and two campground areas. As you ascend a short, steep hill, a gray barn on the right displays a large engraved map of the park directly on the barn wall. Park here or nearby. The trail begins to the left of the barn at a road just beyond two pit toilets.

Elm Brook Park, Hopkinton Dam
West Hopkinton/Weare
8,000 Acres

Recommended walk: Elm Brook
Nature Trail, 1 1/4 miles (loop),
1 hour 30 minutes

An identification trail that skirts Elm Brook Pool, part of the Hopkinton-Everett Lake flood control project.

The dam-created lake alongside this trail adds a pleasant dimension. The Elm Brook Park complex, one of five United States Army Corps of Engineers dams in the Merrimack River basin, offers a tree-ringed lake, a wide swimming beach, and this enjoyable pathway, which starts to the left of the parking lot as you approach the beach.

Enter the trail by stepping through a breach in a low stone wall; a few feet away a box contains the trail guides. Pick up an "Elm Brook Nature Trail" booklet, and begin the walk to the right, following yellow and green blazes. Right away you'll notice that these old, gentle, roomy white pines have a gardenlike feeling to them.

Some of the best advice for this and any walk is found in the guidebook's passage about the first stop,

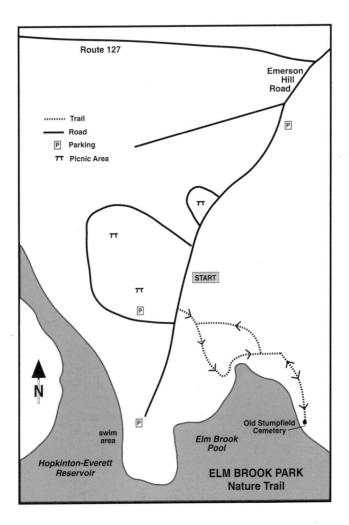

which suggests the purpose of the trail is to strengthen perceptions of the natural world. "As you walk the trail," the guide says, "try to use all of your senses to notice the many details of a natural area. Feel changes in the air, look for signs of wildlife, listen for the many different bird songs, and smell the aroma of the woodland flowers. Although none of these is obvious, you may be surprised by what you find if you try."

As you move slightly downward and continue to the right, the trail takes you in sight of Hopkinton-Everett Reservoir with all its attendant grasses along the shore. This artificial lake is a reservoir completed in 1963. About one mile to the west lies the Hopkinton Dam, which measures 790 feet long, 76 feet high, 378 feet wide at the base, and 24 feet at the top. It was constructed to hold 23 billion gallons. After the severe floods of 1936 and 1938 ravaged Concord, Manchester, Nashua, and surrounding communities, this and other control projects were built to hold back floodwaters from the Contoocook and Merrimack rivers. In April 1987 two back-to-back heavy rainstorms filled the reservoir to 95 percent capacity. The flooding that spring was so severe that standing 50 feet from what is now the shore you would have been under 10 feet of water.

The edge of the lake is to your right, and the trail skirts the shoreline. A short side path leads you into the thickets and bulrushes that line the shore. (Bulrushes, some of which grow to ten feet tall, are named for their long "bullwhip" stems.) A half-trunk on two logs serves as a bench where we sat and watched the

Water lilies grow in profusion and can be seen in many ponds and channels throughout New Hampshire.

red-winged blackbirds vie for territorial rights in the tall grasses.

Returning to the woods, the trail winds through the marshy, sometimes wet, spillover of the lake. This is a good place to identify well-known ferns: the tall royal fern with wide-spaced fronds; the triangular sensitive fern easily spotted in early fall because it turns brown and dies after a light frost; the marsh fern with its wide-spaced pinnae. Wild blue flag iris grow around here too, usually in circular clumps with their roots in or near the water. Sticktights (beggarweeds) with small, orange, basketlike blooms are in evidence trailside as you delve deeper into the woods.

Proceeding, you'll see scattered shelter boxes nailed to tree trunks, referred to in the guide as station 5. These are intended for "cavity dwellers"—the eastern bluebird, tree swallow, gray squirrel, barred and saw-whet owl, and bats—and are used to help protect the young from predators.

Contrary to popular belief, bats are valuable to have around. One small brown bat can eat up to 600 mosquitoes an hour. In fact, bat roosting is encouraged as an alternative to chemical pesticides in many parks and forests.

As you move down the pine needle trail and cross a few log bridges over squishy areas, watch your step on exposed roots. They can be slippery; better to step over than on them.

At the halfway point of the loop, a sign directs you to a side trail on the right (about 450 yards long) to the Old Stumpfield Cemetery, now a pleasant, grassy, lakeside clearing. Follow this flat trail through the woods, cross a footbridge over a rocky brook flowing into a lake channel, turn to the right on the other side, and walk to the end of the cleared section. When the flood control project was built in the 1960s, the old cemetery had to be relocated to dry ground. Now this strip of land is managed as an edge habitat where raspberry, blackberry, and other berries and grasses provide food and cover for animals. Edge dwellers—deer, ruffed grouse, and gray squirrel, to name a few—live well where field and forest meet. Here too is where you'll get a long view down the channel toward the main part of Elm Brook Pool.

Return over the same Stumpfield side trail and turn right when you reach the main loop trail. About 200 yards later remain on the main trail as you meet a Y junction with a cross trail. Soon you pass a large, four-trunk pine on the right. Continue down a slight incline to the starting point.

Getting There

From U.S. 202 and Route 9 in West Hopkinton, drive 2.7 miles north on Route 127 as it turns past the Papertech/Biotech plant and a covered bridge. Entrance signs to Elm Brook Park are on the right in a small residential area. The trail begins on the left about 0.25 mile from the toll booth. The beach and parking lot are in sight at the end of the access road.

Everett Lake Dam
Weare
8,245 Acres

Recommended walk: Everett Lake Dam
Walk, 1 1/2 miles, 1 hour 15 minutes

---

*After a striking view from the dam, you walk on an open
dirt road along a popular recreational lake.*

An exhilarating feature of this site is that at the outset
you stand on top of the high dam and get a wonderful
view of the lake and surrounding forests. On the right
side of the lake lies the irregular shoreline and the
tree-and-grass picnic area of Clough State Park, on the
left the straight-line, dirt road trail to your destination—a short, wooded point jutting into the lake.

Everett Lake Dam is one of five Merrimack River
basin dams that control floodwaters near the three
main cities of Nashua, Manchester, and Concord.
Together with Hopkinton Dam (to which it is connected by a United States Army Corps of Engineers canal),
the two reservoirs have a total holding capacity of 50
billion gallons of water.

Park your car alongside the pass-through fence
gate to the top of the dam, then walk across the 115-
foot-high, 0.5 mile-long dam of the Piscataquog River
(not to be confused with the Piscataqua River in
Portsmouth, New Hampshire).

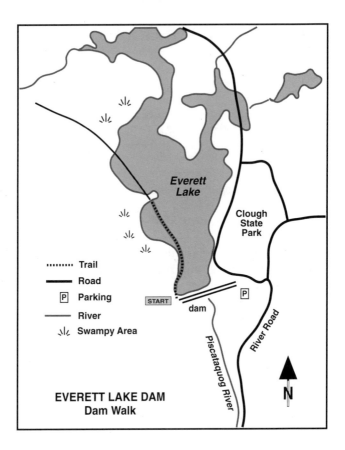

Trail ....
Road ━━━
Parking P
River ───
Swampy Area ∿

Everett Lake

Clough State Park

START

dam

P

Piscataquog River

River Road

N

EVERETT LAKE DAM
Dam Walk

When we visited, project manager Dave Shepardson was at the gatehouse and invited us in to look at the operating room for the hydraulic system. He also opened the hatch in the floor for us to peer down the

United States Army Corps of Engineers projects include many attractive day parks and nature trails.

silolike, several-story control tower, which is partly submerged during floods but remains dry inside. Three three-by-five-feet steel gates open and close to control water flow. In the major flood of 1987 this reservoir system operated at 95 percent of its holding capacity.

A few yards in front of the dam, logs stretch in an arc across the lake. These "boom logs" have been assembled to prevent grass, branches, dead animals, and other debris from clogging the gates. Blue herons find them an excellent place to perch and fish.

At the far end of the dam the paved road also ends. Here you will find a plaque with statistics about the dam. Turn to your right and descend an embankment on a sand road along Everett Lake. Quaking aspen and gray birch grow in the poor soil of the slope. Identify the birch by their extremely fine-notched, pointed leaves; by contrast, aspen leaves are rounder, silver-backed in the sunlight, and of course "quake" even in the softest breeze.

As you walk, notice the plash of water tumbling over the dam sluice. During summer, you'll probably also hear voices of sunbathers and picnicking families from Clough State Park beach across this wide river pool. Fishermen also use this road, taking a few steps onto sandy promontories where they can cast for golden lake perch, small bass, pickerel, and brown trout.

Wildflowers, swamp alders, and viburnum are abundant along the shoreline. Fleabane, with its tiny, daisylike flowers, nods among the grasses of a backwater to the left of the trail, which continues straight and flat between Everett Lake on the right and the intriguing, marshy backwater on the left. Sounding very human, frogs utter tiny alarmed cries and plunk under lily pad cover if you disturb their solitude.

The road continues past a pine-covered peninsula thrusting into the lake. You can't continue on the road because military exercises take place in the area far beyond this point.

Instead, walk onto the peninsula. Substantial white pines somehow have managed to take root on this high sandy knoll. They provide welcome shade from the open road on a sunny day as well as a resting spot for observing wildlife on the lake. Follow the trail back to the dam and across to your car.

A resident Canada goose, who lost its mate, lives on the lake year-round. You may hear its sad honking or even get quite close to the territorial bird if it flies

This resident Canada goose at Clough State Park lost his mate and has since bonded with a park maintenance vehicle.

over to check you out. We were told that the goose has bonded with an orange park service pickup truck, following it everywhere in the Clough beach area.

Getting There

From Manchester drive west on Route 114 past Goffstown to Parker. Turn right on River Road through Riverdale following signs to Clough State Park. Pass the park entrance on the right. Everett Lake Dam is approximately 0.75 mile beyond the park, also on the right. The gates to the dam are closed when the office is unoccupied. But a convenient pass-through opening has been constructed for walkers and fishermen. Park on the roadside.

Silk Farm Wildlife Sanctuary
Concord
15 Acres

Recommended walk: Turkey Pond
Trail, 1 1/2 miles (loop), 45 minutes

A multiuse natural area with good birding from an open boardwalk on Great Turkey Pond.

The Audubon Society maintains thirty wildlife sanctuaries spread through all ten counties of New Hampshire. The trails at Silk Farm (headquarters in Concord), are heavily used. Established in 1972, the Silk Farm Audubon House centralizes their offices and educational programs. On the first floor a nature-oriented gift shop sells items from hand-carved birdbaths to children's waterbird whistles. Here you also may purchase a guide to the Silk Farm property as well as other areas in the state with maintained trail systems.

Of the three trails here, this one takes you, by way of a short boardwalk, directly onto the pond. To get onto Turkey Pond Trail, start at the kiosk to the left of the parking lot. Take the yellow-blazed trail to the right. For a short while it coincides with the red-blazed Forest Floor Trail, then it splits off to the right. In spring this trail glitters with galaxies of starflowers, eastern columbine, and especially the common six-inch-high

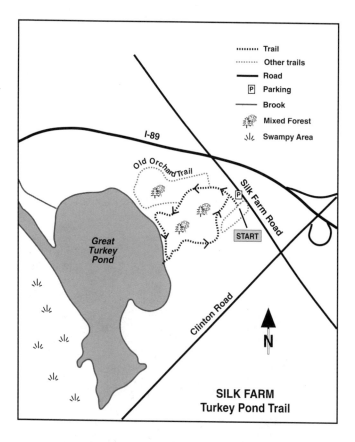

Canada mayflower with its scant two or three broad shiny leaves and single vertical cluster of white flowers (this is also known as false lily of the valley or Massachusetts mayflower). Black-and-white warblers flit through the spring buds as well as sparrow-sized, olive-colored ovenbirds, which look like wood thrushes but wear instead an orange stripe on their crowns, dots on their breasts, and make dome nests from leaf litter (hence their name).

Continue straight at a T junction. About 100 feet later at a Y junction bear right, walking beside a stone wall and through white pine forest. The hurricane of 1938 felled a lot of trees in New Hampshire and many of them were stored at Great Turkey Pond. With Yankee practicality, two sawmills were built in short order to salvage the logs and turn them into profitable lumber.

Arrowheads, lily pads, and reeds like these are found growing at the edge of many ponds.

At the end of the stone wall veer left through a patch of small leafed, bushlike swamp oaks. About 200 feet from the end of the stone wall, the Old Orchard Trail enters from the right; continue straight ahead. The trail widens as it descends gradually through hardwoods and then more steeply down to the edge of the pond. Walk about 200 yards along the boggy shoreline. Notice how the shoreline is grown in with spear-leafed pickerelweed. These deep green water plants predominate in ponds across New Hampshire. Slender pickerel fish lend their name to the dense aquatic plants because they find the weeds ideal for spawning.

A slight jog to the right leads to a boardwalk observation platform. When we visited, bright red cranberries bobbed in the moss underfoot. Many boggy areas such as this offer the perfect habitat for these tart native berries, which ripen at the same time as the fall leaves turn, about six weeks before Thanksgiving.

With a pair of binoculars, you can focus on waterfowl, waders, and other pond inhabitants. You might see mallards, pintails, great blue herons, and Canada geese.

We startled a flock of common mergansers as we negotiated a short stone footbridge through the swampy growth of reeds. Sixty bird species have been sighted at Great Turkey Pond and its neighbor to the north Little Turkey Pond (Turkey River connects the two ponds).

After returning to the main trail, walk only a few yards away from the pond before making a sharp left over a rocky spillway, and then continue through a forest of second-growth mixed woods. In spring look for vernal pools formed by spring rains. In these woodland pools wood frogs, red-backed salamanders, red efts (which look like miniature salamanders), and American toads raise their young free from the threat of fish predators.

A gradual ascent leads to a herd of elephantine boulders on the right. Continue straight and follow the yellow blazes (not the red-blazed trail to your right). After about 200 yards you'll come to a crossroad intersecting the trail near where you started. Turn right and follow the trail a short distance to the parking lot.

Before leaving, we highly recommend that you walk around to the side of the house to the bird coop housing two barred owls. They were injured when young and so can't be released into the wild. For several years the owls have been part of Audubon Society school educational programs. The owls, true to their nature, may be sleeping in the daytime, so don't disturb them. But this handsome male and female pair will be a treat for youngsters and adults alike.

Ruth Smith, Series Program Naturalist, wears thick leather gloves when handling the owls, for though their wings are clipped, their sharp talons and beaks remain in excellent working order. These soft, puffy-headed, gray-brown birds may be identified by white streaked chests and a distinct nocturnal "hoo-hoo hoo-hoo," quartet of hoots.

This injured barred owl is now used for educational purposes by the New Hampshire Audubon Society.

Getting There

From I-93 in Concord take the exit for I-89 and turn at exit 2 onto Clinton Street. Follow well-marked signs to the New Hampshire Audubon Center north on Silk Farm Road. There's ample parking right at the door of the Audubon House.

Southeast
New Hampshire

Merrimack River Outdoor Education and Conservation Area
East Concord
90 Acres

Recommended walk: Les Clark Nature Trail, 1^1/$_4$ miles (loop), 1 hour 15 minutes

---

A captivating exploration of the Merrimack River floodplain below the headquarters of the Society for the Protection of New Hampshire Forests.

The Pemigewasset and Winnipesaukee rivers of central New Hampshire join in the north to form the broad Merrimack River. The Merrimack then flows south 110 miles through New Hampshire and Massachusetts to the Atlantic Ocean. This walk traverses a floodplain of the river, where flatland is subject to flooding but in turn is enriched with thick topsoil. Major flooding is now being held in check by strategic dams and reservoirs near Concord. Editor and conservationist Les Clark (1916–1992) enjoyed walking the Merrimack floodplain, and this self-guided trail was

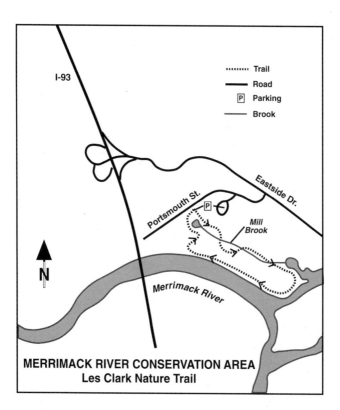

MERRIMACK RIVER CONSERVATION AREA
Les Clark Nature Trail

blazed in his memory. This attractive, many-faceted trail passes through new and old tree farms; past backwaters, channels, and marshes; and along the high, open riverbank. The 17-station "Les Clark Nature Trail" guidebook is available at the office and the kiosk at the beginning of the trail.

The Les Clark Nature Trail stretches along the floodplain of the Merrimack River near Concord.

To get to the trail, walk down a series of more than 100 steps and platforms found to the right of the learning center of the Society for the Protection of New Hampshire Forests. Flowers, trees, and bushes are identified with small tags throughout the area. For example, a sign identifies the prolific Christmas ferns covering the steep embankment. These 1- to 1.5-foot shiny-leafed evergreens have lobed basal blades (pinnae) shaped like miniature Christmas stockings.

At the bottom of the steps turn left onto a wide path. Tall reedy horsetails, relatives of ferns, proliferate here. They grow three to five feet high with straight, upright stems a half inch in diameter and look like dark green miniature bamboo. As children, we used to amuse ourselves by popping apart the segmented hollow stems of these exotic plants. Natives of the Northwest boiled horsetail roots for hair wash, and many tribes used the abrasive stalks for scouring pads to clean mussels and other foods.

Cross a wooden footbridge over Mill Brook and wind past prickly barberry and resilient, willowy osier bushes to a kiosk telling about the trail.

Some of the 17 identifications in the guide booklet refer to general characteristics of floodplains. For instance, trees such as red and silver maple prefer moist soil while shagbark hickories, ash, and basswood seek drier ground. River bottomland usually is prime for farming. This particular ninety-acre tract proves profitable to the Forest Society with its cash crop Christmas tree plantation. Proceeds further conservation work in the state.

Walk along the periphery of the Scotch pine tree farm and past tangled Siamese bittersweet vines (with yellow berries) and elegant, tall ostrich ferns. The ferns (to the left of the trail) have fronds that taper to small appendages at the base of the stem, much like the plume of an ostrich. In early spring, their baby curled shoots—called fiddleheads—are sold in produce sections of many southern New Hampshire markets.

The wetlands of the Merrimack River give refuge to ducks, herons, and other large waders and waterfowl, but the habitats on this walk are varied enough to fit the needs of a number of animals. For instance, next the trail passes through widely spaced meadow pines—quite different in appearance from other pines. Full sunshine has allowed them to spread out and take on the rounded bushy shapes ideal as cover for grouse, rabbit, skunk, and smaller creatures.

Another dirt road loops around to the left, but continue straight ahead and through the sandy, open pasture. Close inspection of the trail might reveal hoofprints. At dawn and dusk this is a good spot to observe browsing rabbits and deer.

Another covered legend and an arrow point out where the trail jags sharply to the left through a mowed meadow, a reminder that though at times the trail seems isolated, it is an urban footpath of Concord. We saw several people walking unleashed dogs, a highly discouraged practice that undoubtedly keeps wildlife wary and hidden during the busier parts of the day.

Turn right and walk along the top of the eroded riverbank through a copse of airy silver maples, then near a dense stand of white pines where yellow-shafted flickers glide among the branches naturally pruned by the crowded struggle for sunshine and growth. The topaz-colored Merrimack River meanders slowly on its way. Emerald grass streams in the lethargic current and glistens in the sunlight.

At an expansive clearing a sign points to another parking lot below the center. Continue along the top of the riverbank past an imposing green ash felled by a hurricane. The sculpted bark and stark polished branches lie silhouetted against the sky. Beyond the green ash, turn right at a gate and walk through the tunneled boughs of a pine plantation laid out prior to Forest Society ownership. These trees are no longer viable as a timber crop. However, their graceful arcades and stately trunks add a cool, vaulted dimension to the trail.

The plantation includes red and white pines. A pine weevil infestation killed most leading buds of the white pine, and as a result many side branches deformed the trees with crooks and forks. A few of the white pines have been pruned to eliminate lower branches. Such pruning helps produce knot-free lumber. Red pines ordinarily aren't valuable timber, but since these weren't attacked by the weevil, they'll make good poles and posts.

Well-managed plantations and woodlots provide a stable source of income for New Hampshire and its residents. Thus, the protection of the forests is vital not only for the preservation of wildlife but for the economic health of the state. In a pamphlet about their award-winning, solar-heated offices and learning center, the Forest Society describes its commitments. One of their goals is "to protect New Hampshire's renewable natural resources through education and practical use."

Turn right at the end of this pine plantation. Proceed on the trail to the yellow double blazes and turn left onto a road. Station 14 identifies a prominent large-crowned shagbark hickory.

Turn right into dense woods. Station 15 indicates a once-active beaver pond, although beavers sometimes return to reactivate a pond. When we were there, beaver activity had ceased and the land was taking over. This is an excellent example of how beaver change a landscape by killing trees with high water levels, developing larger edges for plants and animals as well as providing insect food for many species of birds, especially wood-peckers. These dead trees make good, open bird perches while the woodpeckers' cavities are used later as nests for birds and flying squirrels. Mill Brook, a tributary of the Merrimack, supplies emergent vegetation (plants with roots in the water) for beaver colonies living along the river. Beaver engineering constantly reinvents ponds, pools, and emerging vegetation.

At the trail's end, in a more extensive backwater, you are more likely to sight a beaver, muskrat, or otter. In addition, great blue herons and other waders fish among the purple-flowered pickerelweed and seek camouflage behind buttonbush shrubs with white-ball flower clusters that give the plant its name.

Follow yellow blazes around the end of the pond to a paved road. Turn right and follow the road a short distance to the lower parking lot. Walk through the parking lot and around a green gate. Reenter the trail, which leads back to the steps up to the conservation and learning center.

Getting There

In East Concord, driving north on Interstate 93 take exit 16 and drive 0.8 mile on Eastside Street. Make a sharp right turn onto Portsmouth Drive. Continue 0.2 mile to the conservation center access road and visitors' parking. Forest Society signs are placed at the I-93 exit and on the road.

Northwood Meadows
State Park
Northwood
663 Acres

Recommended walk: Inner Meadow
Pond Trail, 1 1/2 miles (loop), 1 hour

A newly developed trail over varied terrain big, quiet, and dramatic enough for everyone.

Northwood Meadows State Park is a new outdoor delight off busy Route 202/4 east of Concord. The Inner Meadow Pond Trail here has appealing woods. Its most outstanding feature though, is that one day many parts of this trail will be wheelchair accessible. We were fortunate to discover this park early in its development and could see the thought and work going into it.

At one time intended for a housing project, the park is now a partnership of the state of New Hampshire and the Telephone Pioneers of America, which with 825,000 members is the largest industry-sponsored volunteer organization in the world. The trail is designed for the general public, including chair hikers, mountain bikers, and fisherman.

The day we arrived, Norman Harrison, who spearheaded the project, explained that 350 Pioneer volunteers, spending 10,000 hours of work, were

Meadow Pond at Northwood Meadows State Park.

working on a five-year schedule. Although they were still cutting and preparing Inner Meadow Pond Trail, the trail is now open. Enthusiasm is high.

Volunteer Jim Dimick and his daughter Susan gave us a tour of the rough trail as it looped through the woods and along the edge of Meadow Pond. He pointed out areas where grades and surfaces are being built to meet national wheelchair specifications.

That day a small tractor with a rake was leveling the pathway and removing roots. Volunteers were filling potholes with rocks, over which a hardened sandy clay mixture was spread and compacted to even the grade.

Follow the trail to the left parallel to the shore. The trail crosses a brook that feeds the pond. Volunteers

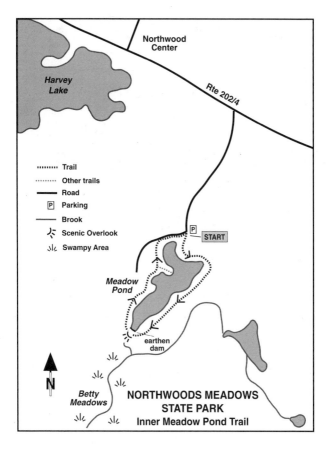

Legend:
- .... Trail
- .... Other trails
- ▬▬ Road
- P Parking
- ── Brook
- ⅄ Scenic Overlook
- ⅃⅃ Swampy Area

Northwood Center

Rte 202/4

Harvey Lake

P START

Meadow Pond

earthen dam

N

Betty Meadows

NORTHWOODS MEADOWS
STATE PARK
Inner Meadow Pond Trail

split logs from timber cut off park land and laid them
across the brook as a foundation. After smoothing the
bridge surface, two-inch-high railings were installed
along the edges of the bridge to keep wheelchairs from

Members of the Telephone Pioneers prepare the trail for wheelchair access.

mishaps. Close by, access paths and special platforms are stationed at pond edge for anyone who wishes to fish in this peaceful setting.

The trail moves up a slight incline and curves through the pines a few yards from shoreline. The trail joins an old dirt road and follows it awhile. Along this section take a close look at a duck house on a pole in the pond. Volunteers are making bat houses with slit entrances on the bottom (that's how bats like to enter). Bats greatly reduce bugs and mosquitoes in the area.

At a Y junction with another road, veer to the right keeping near the shoreline; do the same with a second road, coming in on the left. Continue straight on the trail when the road ends.

As the trail steers ahead onto a narrow, elevated strip of wooded land, it leads to a long viewpoint overlooking a drainage meadow. Make a sharp U bend to the right around the other side of this land strip and descend it about 100 feet to the open end of the pond and the top of a dam.

Turn left and cross the 35-foot-high earth dam to reach the road on the other side. Turn right. While the first half of the trail has wound through woods, this second half skirts the open edge of the pond most of the way, lined predominantly with low alder and scrub brush. It's a good area to spot flickers and blue jays. This pondside stretch adds a lovely dimension to the trail.

Reenter the woods for a brief time. A Y junction leads right to the water's edge. The left fork leads up slightly to a dirt road. Turn right on the road and follow it uphill to an intersection with the main access road; turn right to return to the log cabin center.

Too much activity was going on when we were there to spot wildlife, but Jim said that deer, beaver, and a resident moose have been sighted.

Note: Until this park is fully staffed and the visitor center built near the Inner Meadow Pond trailhead, you may have to walk in via the access road. Check with the state parks department to learn about current wheelchair accessibility.

Getting There

From the Northwood Town Hall on Route 202/4 east of Concord, drive 0.3 mile to the entrance on the right. The access road is 0.6 mile to the junction. Veer left to trailhead.

Bear Brook State Park

Allenstown

9,600 Acres

Recommended walk: Pioneer Nature
Trail, $1/4$ mile (loop), 20 minutes

---

*A booklet-guided trail passing a delightful brook in a rocky
woodland.*

For such a short walk, the Pioneer Trail winds through
an engrossing variety of human and natural history.
At the halfway point, be sure to take a short detour to
visit an enchanting brook burbling over moss-covered
boulders.

The trail begins at the end of an asphalt road in
the park maintenance yard and leads between the
nature center and the park carpentry shop. The trailhead (a dirt road) and "Pioneer Trail" sign are located
at the edge of the woods close to a picnic table and
parking space. Guide booklets are available at the
trailhead or in the nature center.

The large flat area where the maintenance yard
and trailhead are located resulted from outwashes of
streams created by melting glaciers 10,000 years ago.
The flowing water left a sand base here 60 feet thick.

After passing station 1 at hefty white pines, turn
right a short distance later and follow the square yellow blazes onto a footpath. The trail ambles among

This trailhead leads to a short identification trail near Bear Brook State Park, the largest state park in New Hampshire.

young trees, including white oaks with their long, rounded-edge leaves. The spaciousness of the woods invites ground covers such as Canada mayflower to flourish. Canada mayflower, with its broad, strong green leaves, somewhat resembles the lily of the valley, a lily family member that's also a low, creeping perennial. The white flower clusters of the Canada mayflower grow upright; the bell-like, fragrant white flowers of the lily of the valley hang downward. Canada mayflower is also called false (or wild) lily of the valley, two-leaved Solomon's seal, and elf feather.

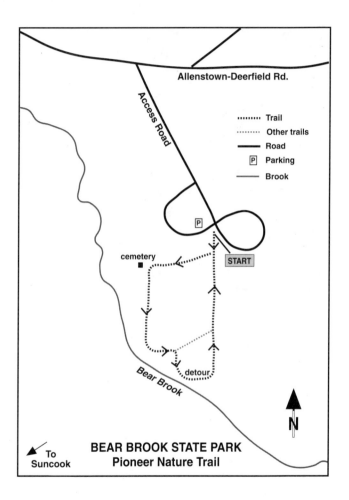

Allenstown-Deerfield Rd.

Access Road

······· Trail
······· Other trails
⸻ Road
P Parking
⸺ Brook

P

cemetery ■

START

Bear Brook

detour

N

To
Suncook

BEAR BROOK STATE PARK
Pioneer Nature Trail

Continue straight on thick pine needle carpeting. The pre–Civil War cemetery of the Johnson and Clark families appears among post–Civil War trees. Granite posts and wrought iron fencing remain from the family plot of this early homestead.

The trail turns left at the cemetery and continues past more evident ground cover, including golden thread with small, dark green leaves that have a thin "gold" line down the center and red berries. Trailing tree club moss, another ground cover, looks like pine seedlings but isn't. You'll likely see bunchberry with its four-petal white flower (producing red berries in summer) against six leaves that resemble a miniature dogwood (it's a member of the dogwood family). We saw a few starflowers too, with long, narrow, pointed leaves in a star burst resting on a thin, foot-high stem. Partridgeberry, with pairs of opposite leaves on a stem capped with two white flowers, is named for the ruffed grouse (or partridge) that eats the winter berries.

When the trail reaches another left turn, look for a short detour (yellow and red blazes) to Bear Brook. The scene will enchant the socks off you (if you want to refresh your feet). This hemlock-shaded spot shows how moss thrives in moist, sunless ravines. Besides being soft underfoot, mosses are highly useful as water retainers, soil anchors, and soil makers. Continue on the trail as it circles left, rejoins the main trail, and soon turns onto the same dirt road at the trailhead. In the last century this road was a county thoroughfare to Candia and passed the Cate family farmstead, now only an overgrown cellar hole (on the left about 100 feet after rejoining the road).

Walk straight back toward the entrance. Along the way look for more wildflowers in a small clearing. Cinquefoil (named for the five leaves and five flowers after "cinque" from the French) is plentiful. Meadowsweet, with its vertical, pink, aromatic flower cluster, is less abundant. The clearing was used by Girl Scouts as a campsite for nearly two decades until 1968.

A prominent stand of red pine on your right shows at a glance how the rust-colored bark got its name. Red pine needles cluster in pairs.

The trailhead is a short distance ahead.

Getting There

From Suncook (between Manchester and Concord) take Route 28 north to Allenstown. Turn right on the Allenstown-Deerfield Road. Drive 1 mile to a toll booth (nominal fee charged) in Bear Brook State Park. Turn right here into the maintenance yard and drive a short distance straight back to the end where the Pioneer Trail begins. Parking is free here.

Bear Brook State Park

Allenstown

9,600 Acres

Recommended walk: Beaver Pond
Trail, 2 miles (loop), 1 hour

---

*A charming stroll encircling a wooded pond and passing
through an intriguing marsh grass shoreline.*

In this section of Bear Brook State Park you'll find
developed campsites in nicely pruned woods; a small,
open playing field; a cozy swimming beach; and an
intriguing bird-filled marsh.

The yellow-blazed trail takes you all the way
around Beaver Pond, with water in sight nearly the
entire route. Except for a short pass over a rock outcrop, the well-maintained, clearly marked path
remains relatively flat.

From parking spaces near the beach, begin by
crossing the sand beach. Walk past a shed on the left
and enter the trail, which is to the right of a road that
enters the woods. About twenty feet from the beach a
bright yellow arrow marks the trailhead.

We enjoy Beaver Pond Trail most in the off-season, when fewer visitors are found along the beach
and trail. Even in the crowded summer season,
though, the forested shore offers a sense of relaxing
isolation.

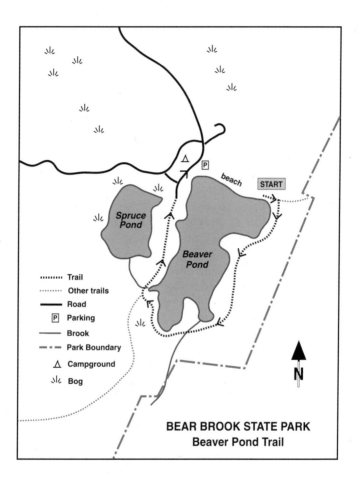

START

beach

Spruce
Pond

Beaver
Pond

.... Trail
.... Other trails
——— Road
P Parking
——— Brook
—··— Park Boundary
△ Campground
☀ Bog

N

BEAR BROOK STATE PARK
Beaver Pond Trail

White pines carpet the trail with needles. In a short time you pass through waist-high huckleberry bushes. If it's late summer, these larger, darker cousins of blueberries will be ripe. So many bushes line the way that the trail seems misnamed; you'll definitely see more huckleberries than beaver.

Along the south side of the pond, the route passes within a few yards of the water. Short access paths allow you to walk to the pond edge.

After clearing a slight rise, the reddish bark of Norway pines catches your eye. On the left an abrupt, dark, rocky upthrust runs parallel to the trail a short distance. Double yellow blazes are used on this trail to indicate either a sharp turn in the trail ahead or a junction with another trail. When the double blazes appear, take the trail to the right, which leads you around the boggy section of the pond. Boardwalks help keep feet dry; the trail looks low enough to flood in spring. The terrain at the end of the pond is wet and requires a series of footbridges and boardwalks.

Finally, you enter slightly higher ground and move onto a lumber tote road. A working lumber road can be disconcerting when you're on a nature walk: balloon tractor tire tracks in the topsoil, ripped and gouged logs lying askew, open wounds in the earth. On the other hand, sensible selective logging with enlightened practices of renewable commercial forestry can be consistent with the impressive array of paper products and by-products available. In fact, working toward a forestry that is concerned with an ample natural world to walk in and still produce paper on which you're reading this (and the extraordinary plethora of other products) is an honorable goal for both producer and consumer.

Turn right on the lumber road, which turns right and back into the woods. The trail takes you through many interesting sections at this shrub-thick end of the pond, including an avenue of ferns four feet high.

Soon another section of the trail crosses a long log footbridge of railroad ties laid in swamp mud. This is a mesmerizing spot to linger. Spiky, torchlike cattails grow among the scrub brush and spiny gorse thickets, where shy warning chirps of nearby hidden birds mix with impudent shrills of red-winged blackbirds. Caretakers Phil and Joyce Carr tell us that loons have been spotted on the pond.

As you move away from the southern end of the pond, follow the trail along the other side. The trail regains its wide and dry texture, and the woods are big and airy again. Watch for a big white pine on the left growing from a horizontal fissure in a boulder. Here grow a few sweet ferns, their dark green, smooth-scalloped, very narrow fronds growing in small, short clumps.

At a T junction, turn right. Spruce Pond shines through the trees on the left.

At a second T junction go left, following a big yellow arrow. Soon the campground and the asphalt road appear. Campsite 63 on the right is the first one you'll see. Ahead a short distance turn right opposite the rest rooms and walk through the campground, across a playing field, and past more campsites to the road that leads you back to the beach.

Getting There

From Suncook (between Manchester and Concord) take Route 28 north to Allenstown. Turn right on the Allenstown-Deerfield Road. Drive 1 mile to a toll booth (nominal fee charged) in Bear Brook State Park. On the same road continue another 1.6 miles to the park campground entrance. Take the main access road to the camp store, following signs to the campground. Steer to the left of the store and about another 0.25 mile to the Beaver Pond beach.

Bear Brook State Park

Allenstown
9,600 Acres

Recommended walk: Smith Pond
Shelter Trail, 1 mile, 45 minutes

---

*A short, sweet trail through spacious pines to a picturesque
marsh and cozy park shelter.*

Sometimes you feel like walking a short way on effortless flat terrain to a picturesque bog where you can sit
and stare and just plain while the hour away. This
walk is one of them. For its simplicity and accessibility
to the entrance road, we found this trail quietly exhilarating, especially the sense of being *in* the woods and
still *seeing* the woods.

You can begin the walk at two trailheads. The first
(labeled X-C 4, referring to cross-country skiing trail)
is located directly off the main campground road to
Beaver Pond; look for the sign to the trailhead turnoff
about a half mile past the sign to the archery range.
We took the second trailhead—X-C 5 on the main
campground road—returning about two miles from
the store at Beaver Pond. These two trails join as X-C 6
about 0.3 mile into the woods and in turn lead to the
log shelter at the edge of the Smith Pond bog.

Park by the edge of the road. Follow blazes
through the spacious red pine forest. In spring and

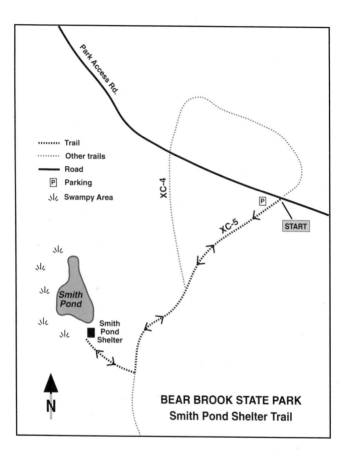

Legend:
.... Trail
.... Other trails
—— Road
P Parking
🌿 Swampy Area

Park Access Rd.

XC-4

XC-5

P

START

Smith Pond

Smith Pond Shelter

N

BEAR BROOK STATE PARK
Smith Pond Shelter Trail

late fall mushrooms push through the thick layer of rust pine needles. We saw giant fungi as large as saucers. Using the mycologists' rule of thumb we checked underneath the cap to see if the mushroom had gills or pores. Those with gills are called agarics; these fungi, which had pores under the cap, were boletes. Spores of the agarics are located on the surfaces of the gills; the spores of the boletes are found in tubes under the cap.

With the rust-colored pine needle carpet and reddish orange tree trunks, the woods have a warm, glowing hue even in the rain. Because of the openness, you will tend to look straight and long, but as in all woods, keep your ears open and eyes on the canopy for dangling, loose pine limbs known as "widow-makers" or "dead men." Whatever you call them, a strong wind can knock one from its perch and send it crashing to the ground.

At the convergence of X-C 4 and X-C 5, X-C 6 continues on, curving gently to the left. A side trail, marked with a "No Camping" sign, leads to the right. Follow this trail about 50 yards to reach the shelter. As lean-tos go, Smith Pond Shelter is a handsome one with a large stone fireplace for day-use hikers and cross-country skiers. These shelters can be lifesavers in harsh weather. The area in front of the Smith Pond Shelter is cleared to reveal the full splendor of the large primeval-looking pond. Sawed beams provide steps down the steep embankment to the boggy pond.

Polished dead pine trunks in the still, dark water reach upward eighty to one hundred feet in stark weathered poses—their witchy branches spread against the sky. They provide momentary roosts for

This lean-to at Smith Pond provides shelter for day hikers and skiers in Bear Brook State Park.

kingfishers, flycatchers, and other birds that feed on insects and fish in this freshwater pond. Take time to make your way down the log-banked sandy slope in front of the shelter to the muddy marsh edge where you can better see the full extent of this primordial scene of murky waters and big, dead trees.

Retrace the trail to return to the parking area.

Getting There

From Suncook (between Manchester and Concord) take Route 28 north of Allenstown. Turn right on the Allenstown-Deerfield Road. Drive 1 mile to a toll booth (nominal fee charged) into Bear Brook State

Although called Smith "Pond," this area is really an extensive marsh with good waterfowl watching.

Park. On the same Deerfield Road continue 1.6 miles to the park campground entrance. Take the main access road past an archery range to your left. Stop at cross-country (X-C) ski trail X-C 5 and park at the trailhead on the right.

Pawtuckaway State Park
Raymond
5,500 Acres

Recommended walk: Fundy Trail
(Burnhams Marsh), 2 miles, 1 hour

A hemlock-sheltered mile-long esplanade with unobstructed views of this active marsh.

A reason Pawtuckaway State Park draws so many people is its varied terrain—large and small ponds, giant marsh, secluded tree-lined coves, mountaintops with panoramic views, backcountry isolation, swimming beach popularity. With 170 tent sites, camp store, canoe rentals, and boat launch access, this is a full-fledged, multipurpose park. Yet despite all the activity, sections of the park, including the area the Fundy Trail passes through, transport you far and wide of people and noise.

This trail takes its name from Fundy Cove, an inlet of Pawtuckaway Lake. However, the most interesting part of the trail is Burnhams Marsh, a mile-long swampy area that bottlenecks midway to form an hourglass. The trail is laid out beneath the cool, sheltering hemlocks that border the open, sunny marsh. This side-by-side juxtaposition makes an enjoyable two-in-one walk.

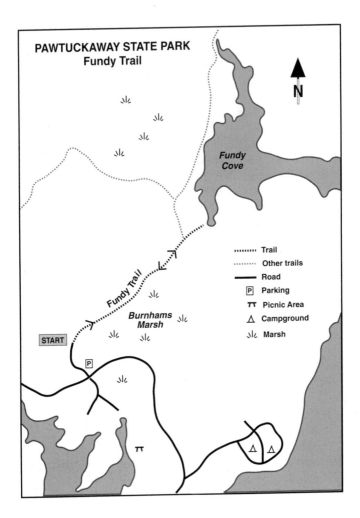

PAWTUCKAWAY STATE PARK
Fundy Trail

Fundy
Cove

Fundy Trail

Burnhams
Marsh

START

P

.... Trail
.... Other trails
———— Road
P   Parking
⊤⊤ Picnic Area
△   Campground
⩊ Marsh

N

After driving about 1.5 miles from the park entrance to the trailhead (marked #3), park by the side of the road. Turn left off the park maintenance road and follow white blazes through quaking aspen on a sandy tote road lined with Scotch pines. Cross a wide plank bridge and enter a tall hemlock stand. Balsam and hemlock branches often were spread beneath the bed sacks of early campers, but in these days of air mattresses and water-resistant pads, cutting is discouraged. Fallen needles make a cushiony path. At first the marsh is scarcely noticeable among the tree branches to your right. Wild sarsaparilla are abundant in this hemlock grove. During the last century these common roots were used as flavor extracts in soft drinks.

The hemlocks soon blend with tall eastern white pines. To the right of the trail, Burnhams Marsh appears in full view. You may observe sunning frogs and basking turtles on dead stumps and logs near the shore. Peer into the dark, punky water. On the surface, water striders dance. Dragonflies dip and light on reeds and rushes. Dead tree stumps are home to flycatchers, kingfishers, and other birds that feed on a cornucopia of flies and other insects. Beaver, deer, and great blue heron may be present but are more likely to be seen at dawn or dusk when they are feeding.

The marsh unfolds myriad secrets to the quiet, patient observer. The shadow of a turkey vulture drifts ominously over the dark water; a chipmunk scrambles from the shore and retires into the safety of the woods. In spring, red-winged blackbirds cluck and trill, perching on the tallest rushes to entice a mate with their high-pitched whistles.

Rushes and other grasses crowd the lower reach of Burnhams Marsh. Beyond the bottleneck, about halfway on the trail, an entirely different marsh environment takes over. Lily pads and algae cover the water, choking out taller growth and creating a more open expanse.

While a marsh has some drainage along with its sedges, cattails, and rushes, a bog usually is undrained or poorly drained with sedges, shrubs, and sphagnum moss, more spongy decayed matter, and a quagmire of mud.

The trail veers left away from the marsh, back into hemlock and mixed woods. You'll pass through an opening in a stone wall and continue over another wide plank bridge before coming to sign #4 , marking the turnoff to the Shaw Trail (the number refers to major features of the park, not a guidebook). The Fundy Trail continues a quarter of a mile to the Fundy Cove boat launch. On our visit we preferred to concentrate on the marsh habitat, which offers ample sights and a wide variety of wildlife. The Burnham's Marsh walk incorporates the best of both worlds: the active sunlit backwater with its croaking frogs and buzzing flies as well as the dark forest with its chattering red squirrels and nuthatches. The going is flat and easy, with enough discoveries to fill the round-trip with continuous new sights and sounds.

Return to the parking area by retracing your path along the Fundy Trail.

A frog suns itself on Burnhams Marsh.

Getting There

On Route 101 east from Manchester take Raymond/Nottingham exit 5 and follow state park signs to Route 156. Drive 2 miles and turn left onto Mountain Road. The park entrance is another 2 miles on the left. Pass through the toll booth and continue on the main park road to marker #3. (Each feature or trail in the park is labeled with a number.) A modest fee is charged.

Pawtuckaway State Park
Raymond
5,500 Acres

Recommended walk: South Mountain
Lookout Tower Trail, 1 mile, 45 minutes

Sky-scraping panoramic views reward an easy summit climb.

The Pawtuckaway State Park is large and sections are undeveloped. The trails are well maintained by the New Hampshire chapter of the Appalachian Mountain Club, but dirt service roads are many, unmarked, ungraded, and sometimes confusing. So tank up and be prepared for some bumpy driving.

If you select a clear day for this walk, from the scenic tower on South Mountain you'll be able to see the coastal Hamptons to the east, Boston to the south, and as far as Grand Monadnock to the southwest.

After parking in a small space to the side of the trailhead, start Lookout Tower Trail to the left of park sign #6, which designates the trailhead, not a station in a guidebook; the trail is marked with white blazes. The trail climbs gradually with hairpin turns up the 908-foot mountain. The walk isn't too strenuous and the trail ascends through scattered beech and white pines. Once in the woods, you'll see massive glacial boulders that tumbled down the mountainside. Called "erratics," they create deep caves for hibernating animals

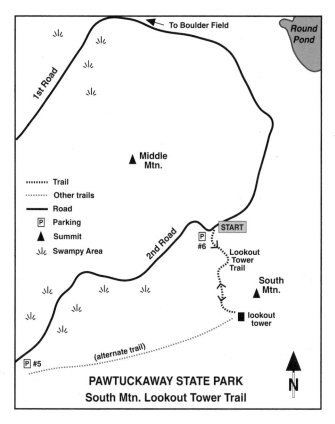

To Boulder Field

1st Road

Round Pond

▲ Middle Mtn.

········· Trail
········· Other trails
——— Road
P Parking
▲ Summit
⚶ Swampy Area

2nd Road

P #6

START

Lookout Tower Trail

South ▲ Mtn.

■ lookout tower

(alternate trail)

P #5

PAWTUCKAWAY STATE PARK
South Mtn. Lookout Tower Trail

N

during the long, cold winter.

After about twenty minutes, you'll crest the mountain, pass a ramshackle empty shed, and reach the base of the fire tower. The tower is open to visitors from early spring through late fall, conditions permitting.

The fire lookout we talked with was informative

A view of the South Mountain fire lookout tower.

and seemed to enjoy company. He told us 10 fire towers were occupied in southern New Hampshire and 6 in the north. The lookout said that the tower system is extremely important in spotting and containing smaller fires. If not caught in time, forest fires can destroy hundreds of acres of valuable timber and wildlife habitats.

North Mountain (Mount Pawtuckaway) is 1,011 feet high. Although South Mountain is a little lower, it has spectacular panoramic views in all directions. On a clear day you can see the light bouncing off the windows in Boston skyscrapers. The expansiveness of Burnham's Marsh and Lake Pawtuckaway with its 700-foot beach also are impressive. As you look from the tower, the green sea of forest fades into the blue horizon.

Turkey vultures coast the thermals. On our way down a chipmunk or two made their presence known, but for the most part wildlife keeps hidden. That's partly because of the human traffic: Despite the isolation of the Tower Trail, it's popular and well traveled. We encountered several families from New York, New Jersey, and New Hampshire.

Once you return to the trailhead you can drive 2.0 miles farther up the dirt road to reach a 0.5-mile-long trail leading through Boulder Field, where the glacial erratics are so high rock climbers practice rappelling off them. Be prepared for a bumpy ride if you decide to visit the boulders. If that's not for you, we suggest letting the breathtaking views from South Mountain crown your day.

Getting There

(This trail is 15 miles from the park entrance.) From exit 5 at Raymond off Route 101 east, turn north onto Business Route 101/27. In 3.8 miles turn right onto Route 107 north. Stay on Route 107 for 3 miles. Turn right onto Reservation Road (after Ruby's Hair Salon, a Pawtuckaway State Park sign is partially hidden by tree foliage in summer and fall). Drive exactly 1.2 miles on Reservation Road. On the left of the road is the sign "Lookout Tower." Reset your odometer. Bear right and drive 1.4 miles. You'll come to park sign #5 (trails and features in the park are numbered) at a narrow dirt road. Turn left. Drive 0.8 mile on a bumpy road to park sign #6. (Note: after heavy rains this road might be impassable. Park at #5 and use this trail to the tower instead.)

Rye Beach
Rye

Recommended walk: Seawall Walk,
1 mile, 30 minutes

A sidewalk stroll along ocean coves in sight of the Isles of Shoals.

Along the seacoast of Rye Beach are wonderful sights, sounds, and, of course, invigorating salt air smells. A few spots to visit on the way to this walk include ever-changing Rye Harbor Marina, where working fishing crews chug in and out of the giant granite block break-water; the small, irresistible Rye Harbor State Park jutting into the ocean; the 700-foot Wallis Sands State Beach; and the many tidewater inlets on the west side of Route 1A. This area (which includes both tiny beach cottages and seashore mansions) retains an open, uncongested "homey" ambiance. We visit here throughout the year for Atlantic Ocean refreshers, but probably the best seasons include the pre- and post-summer weeks.

The Seawall Walk encompasses a large-pebble, shallow cove with glacial stones that were deposited from as far away as the White Mountains during the last Ice Age. Twice in modern times, extreme low tides have uncovered 3,200-year-old cedar stumps in this area, reminders of when the coastline was a wooded

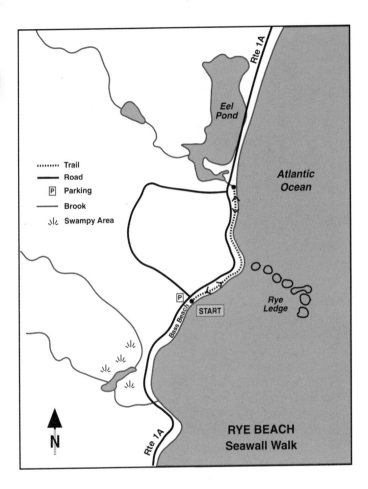

Trail
Road
P Parking
Brook
Swampy Area

Rte 1A

Eel
Pond

Atlantic
Ocean

Rye
Ledge

P
Bass Beach
START

Rte 1A

RYE BEACH
Seawall Walk

N

Herring gulls and friends enjoy roosting on Rye Ledge.

extension of land stretching to the Isles of Shoals. Next to the beach, sofa-size blocks of granite are piled into a state-made breakwater to prevent high waves from flooding the area during intense winter storms.

On a sidewalk next to a seawall parallel to coastal Route 1A, start walking north from Bass Beach. Along the wall you'll see parts of Rye Ledge, a rocky peninsula that juts about 0.25 mile into the sea. Have your binoculars handy because the ledge is a roosting place for gulls, cormorants, and sea ducks. Immature black-headed gulls and black-legged kittiwakes are frequently seen in the air. Nicknamed "the minister" by fishermen, the black-backed gull, with a wingspan of five feet, is the largest nesting gull. A list of more than

141 resident and migrating birds has been compiled for this coastal area.

Rye Ledge is visible only in small sections even at low tide. Marine nomads are fond of it. In early spring we've seen 200-pound golden harbor seals lounging on the ocher-colored shoals and ledges. Golden harbor seals are fin-footed pinnipeds. They have no external ears (sea lions and fur seals do). If you've ever wondered about the function of seal whiskers, you're in good company. Marine scientists haven't reached a definitive conclusion, but some say the whiskers serve as short-range sensing devices that help the seals locate fish and alert them to threatening intruders. Toothed whales and porpoises use echolocation (a sort of sonar), but harbor seals evidently don't have this ability.

To your left as you walk along, you can't miss three curious examples of mansion "cottages" in a row—a gray-shingled Victorian with a white sitting porch, a redbrick Versailles-style display of ultrasymmetrical architecture, and a modern tower house with a bold, pedestaled platform.

The white buildings of the Isles of Shoals stand out on the horizon, about six miles off Rye Beach. Discovered by Captain John Smith in 1614, the Isles have an extraordinary history. Once a predominantly Norwegian fishing community, the Isles (four in New Hampshire, five in Maine) were world renowned for their "dun fish" (dried cod). During the midnineteenth century, poet/writer/gardener Celia Laighton Thaxter invited many literary and artistic luminaries to her island cottage, including Nathaniel Hawthorne and

John Greenleaf Whittier. On Appledore Island of the Isles, guests at her parents' 500-room Appledore Hotel praised and amazed over Celia's beloved flower garden (the hotel burned down in 1914). Her book *An Island Garden,* illustrated by Childe Hassam, is still in print. The garden has been re-created on Appledore Island by the Portsmouth Garden Club. From the seawall you might catch sight of a ferry plying its way to or from the Isles, as well as whale-watching tour boats. Humpback and minke whale pods migrate seasonally east past the Isles.

About halfway along your walk, the sidewalk rises a couple of yards to the top of the seawall and onto a boardwalk. This gives you a low-flying gull's-eye view—but watch your step. The boardwalk shifts slightly underfoot. Alcoves of magenta fireweed and spiky, cylinder-tipped cattails grow across Route 1A. The delicate, white heads of tenacious Queen Anne's lace and the sweet-and-soft-textured beach pea grow along the walk here, too. Although they resemble garden peas, they're toxic.

At the end of the walk, descend the seawall to a parking lot of a private beach club. Bushy rows of beach roses line the oceanfront. These dainty roses flower against deep green foliage throughout the summer, displaying pink and white blossoms and exuding their heady perfume. After blossoming, they transform into rose hips, a ball-like fruit. Rose hips are high in vitamin C and gardeners often pick and dry them, but these are for public display.

Beach roses enhance your walk along the seawall at Rye Beach.

Return the same way to your car. Then if you wish, extend this pleasant walk when you return to your starting point by continuing for about 1.5 miles along the walkway in the opposite direction to enjoy more salt air and seashore.

Getting There

From Route 101 east near Exeter, take Route 111 east to Route 1A. Turn left on Route 1A at the ocean shore and drive about 1.5 miles to a sign on the left: "Abenaqui Country Club/St. Theresa Catholic Church/St. Francis Retreat Center." Park for free in the lot of this abandoned retreat center. Parking is prohibited on Route 1A.

Odiorne Point State Park
Rye
137 Acres

Recommended walk: Odiorne Point
Trail, 1 1/4 miles (loop), 1 hour 15 minutes

---

*A history-laden walk through seven habitats along the pic-
turesque Gulf of Maine.*

This is one of our favorite coastal walks. Once, Odiorne Point was covered by dense ancient cedar forests
that extended ten miles straight out to the Isles of
Shoals, until the last Ice Age dramatically transformed
the landscape. As the ice retreated north it left a jumbled beach scape of sedimentary glacial quartz sand-
stone, shale, and lime rock, scraped off from the land
to the north and deposited here. The park was created
in 1972.

The Odiorne Point Trail starts behind the visitor
center on the ocean side, entering two of the park's
seven different habitats—the Gulf of Maine ocean and
rocky shore intertidal areas. Walk through a tight
canopy of sumac along the shoreline. Through the
foliage you'll glimpse herring gulls and perhaps a cor-
morant spreading its large dark wings to dry out as it
perches on a barnacled ledge.

Short side paths lead to beach beds of kelp and
other sea wrack and tidal pools where, at low tide, you

The tidal area along Odiorne Point is home to the eel-like gunnel fish, starfish, sea urchins, and other small saltwater creatures.

may examine sea urchins, limpets, eel-like gunnel fish, starfish, and other saltwater inhabitants. Tide-line deposits of black matchbook-size hollow skate egg cases, pieces of washed-up finger sponges, and shells left by whelks, blue mussels, and moon snails offer delightful diversions.

A panorama of the Gulf of Maine and Whaleback Lighthouse yields to trees as the trail angles right at a Y junction and past a freshwater marsh. Grape vines cover the chokecherry trees and alder and indicate a source of freshwater nearby.

To the left visitors are accosted by the gaping concrete tunnel entrance to Seaman Battery bulwark, a

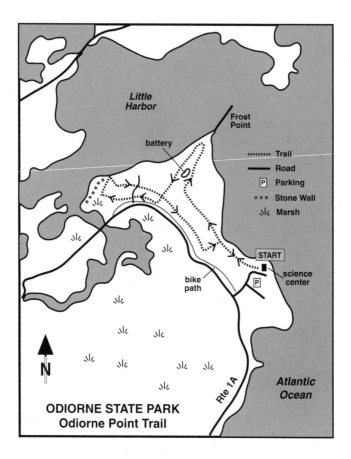

ODIORNE STATE PARK
Odiorne Point Trail

World War II defense for the Portsmouth Navy Shipyard. These long concrete casements are so well camouflaged with earth they look like coastal hills and blend into the tangled vines and burdock undergrowth.

Turn left and walk directly through the battery entrance, then turn right so the bulwark is to your right. Take the right loop to Frost Point. This point was identified by Giovanni da Verrazano in 1524. The first European to settle on this point in 1759 called his farm the Pannaway Plantation. In the nineteenth century, farmland gave way to a rambling ocean-side inn, The Sagamore House; in turn, the inn gave way to Fort Dearborn bunkers.

Wild bright yellow tansy, trailing groundnut, Queen Anne's lace, purple vetch, and other meadow flowers proliferate on the point. So do rabbits. Frequently, they may be seen near their burrows in clearings among the tall grasses at dinnertime. Here the trail loops left around the point, hugging the shore

Rabbits proliferate at Odiorne Point.

with a view of the Wentworth Marina across Little Harbor. If you step off the trail for a raspberry or two, look out for poison ivy—clusters of three smooth, shiny green leaves are your clue.

After looping around, retrace your steps past the last bulwark entrance on your left and then turn right on a graded gravel road. Remain on this road leading to a macadam bike trail that parallels Route 1A. At the bikeway take another right to reach the boat launch. The boat launch fronts another Odiorne Point habitat, the salt marsh. Cordgrass grows out into the water and reaches a height of nine feet, which enables it to absorb light when the tide comes in. Its extensive root system is well anchored in the mud. The shorter species of the *Spartina* grass family grows in clumps on the high tidal periphery. On coastal plantations as far south as the Carolinas, early farmers raked and gathered this "salt marsh hay."

Follow the trail to the right of the launch along a stone tidal wall. You're likely to see an egret or small blue heron fishing for a tasty hermit crab or blue mussel in the marsh grass and poking with its sharp beak into the Atlantic ooze for surf clams and shrimp.

Walk to the end of the wall at the beach. Turn right and enter a well-worn woodland path in a pine and oak forest. Continue through an opening in a stone wall and into a short stand of sumac. You may hear the brassy squawking of blue jays and the crazy-quilt gibberish of catbirds calling back and forth as you continue along a crumbling macadam path through a healthy grove of shagbark hickory around the base of a World War II structure. These trees are easily identified by their broad five-to-seven-leaf clusters and scaly, peeling gray bark.

At all junctions on the way back to the science center, bear left in this crisscross section toward the ocean. The trail makes a slight jog across the graded gravel road you previously walked and enters the woods again. Stately sap maples line this old carriage road, testimony to the manorial estates that once dominated the point. Continue down this straight road until you reach the connecting path to the science center.

By the time you reach the science center, you will have walked through the shore/intertidal area beside the Gulf of Maine, meadow, upland forest, and along the salt marsh.

We often pack a picnic when we visit Odiorne Point State Park. The Atlantic salt air whets the appetite, and picnic tables are spaced along the ocean for spectacular views.

Getting There

From U.S. 1 near North Hampton take Route 111 east to coastal Route 1A. You come out at Little Boar's Head. Turn left onto Route 1A and drive north up the coast about 8 miles. Odiorne Point State Park is on the right. The entrance leads directly to the parking area. A long, wide asphalt walkway leads to the science center. A modest fee is charged in summer.

Urban Forestry Center
Portsmouth
180 Acres

Recommended walk: Brooks Trail,
2 miles, 1 hour

A winding passage through roomy forest to the sparkling saltwater marshes of Sagamore Creek.

John Elwyn Stone (1922–74) put into action his enthusiasm for the stewardship of land and sea by donating his estate for the inspiration and enjoyment of everyone. Stone preserved the site against the encroachment of seacoast city expansion and commercial development. Managed by the New Hampshire Division of Forests and Lands, the Urban Forestry Center offers more than just an agreeable walk through woods and alongside a captivating salt marsh. Stone's estate is now a learning center providing technical guidance on the care of urban trees and shrubs, helping town conservation commissions and land developers with public urban forestry, and other related projects. Programs for the general public include weekly seminars on learning about shrubs and trees that attract backyard birds, field trips, slide shows, historical programs, and other topics, as well as special events on Arbor Day in April, "Forestry Day" in July, and "Festival of Trees" in December.

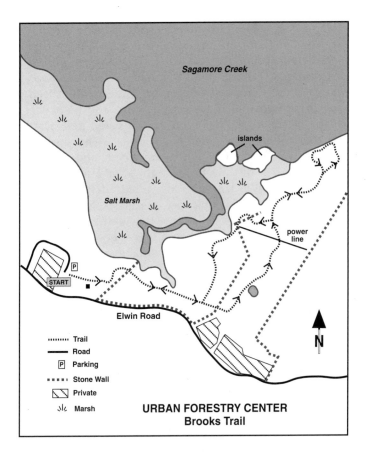

URBAN FORESTRY CENTER
Brooks Trail

Stone's keen sense of looking to the future stemmed from strong family ties to the past. He was a direct descendant of John Langdon (1741–1819), New

Hampshire's first governor, as well as being directly related to Tobias Langdon, who first settled this acreage in 1650.

Brooks Trail leads you through old-growth woods to the tidal marshes of Sagamore Creek. Introduced by a trim row of lilacs on one side and a spruce demonstration plantation on the other, the trail starts at the parking lot in front of the office. After skirting an open field, the trail enters the woods and follows white blazes, turning to the right after a few yards. Here full-grown trees are identified, including fine examples of shagbark hickory, white oak, and American beech with its broadly oval, leathery, clearly veined leaves (in winter beech leaves hold fast to the tree, rustling their buff fall legacies through the snowy months). A little farther on, the black birch on your right shows how broad the birch family is, ranging in color from snow white to golden to black. All birches, including this black one, show characteristic horizontal "Morse code" dots and dashes on the bark. Black birch (also known as sweet or cherry birch) is the source for birch beer. Made from its sap, birch beer is still remembered as emblematic of spring.

To the left of the first section of the trail, parts of a sixty-acre saltwater marsh are visible. The tidal inlet of Sagamore Creek feeds this salt marsh, forming an ecologically valuable buffer zone between land and sea. Here freshwater mixes with salt water, producing an exceptionally varied system of plants, animals, fowl, and fish that share the mix.

As you cross a small drainage gully, you might spot skillet-size pond turtles residing in a backwater to your right.

At the first trail junction (a trail enters left), continue straight uphill, passing nodding deep green Solomon's seal. The trail connects to a dirt road. Go left. Walk down this shaded road a minute or two, then take a sharp left to reach a compact marshy pond on the right, somewhat hidden by roadside brush. This is the kind of primordial pool that brews and supports life in all sizes and forms—frogs, dragonflies, kingfishers, turtles.

Continue down the weedy road past birch and beech saplings. A curious mix of sounds and sights reminds you that this indeed is an urban walk even though you're in a forest. In the distance bell buoys ring, trains whistle, and—up ahead—you cross under a power line. At the same time you might hear nature sounds such as the territorial whirring of red-winged blackbirds, the throaty burps of frogs.

Continue veering to the right as you pass three other trails entering on the left. These are open, gracious woods, but eventually, the trail narrows and the foliage tightens to a single-file path. This signals that you're approaching a point of land where the trail loops to the left, skirting a rocky edge of Sagamore Creek. This designated waterbird observation area is a wonderful spot to stand and stare. Below, shallow sea green water ebbs and flows with the tide. Across the strait, forest and rock line the inlet. On your right, salt marsh grasses stretch to where woods and sky meet and a church steeple pierces the far horizon.

For centuries these marsh grasses were cut and dried for hay. The wetlands were extremely useful and productive but also fragile. Man-made drainage ditches and channels take a generation to repair; use of the marsh is now restricted. Nevertheless, the grasses that a salt marsh produces remain the same—variations of basic *Spartina*. Tall, frilly top cordgrasses grow immediately above the high tide line; shorter marsh hay grows on the high shore.

As you round the point, circle back to the main trail. Before you recross under the power line, look for an arrow blaze on a tree. Take this trail to the right. It leads to a pine needle path through conifers. You will reach an opening by a narrow branch of a tidal inlet, where the salt marsh almost appears at eye level. Once back in the woods, follow an arrow to a junction. From the footbridge look for animal tracks in the mud. We saw otter and raccoon tracks well preserved in the wet soil.

Keep to the right and in less than five minutes of casual walking you'll return to the first section of the trail. Turn right, and return to the starting point.

Getting There

From Interstate 95 in Portsmouth take exit 3 onto Route 101. Turn right onto Elwyn Road to U.S. 1 (Lafayette Road). Continue on Elwyn Road across U.S. 1 for about 0.25 mile. The Urban Forestry Center is on the left and well marked.

Adams Point Wilderness Management Area
Durham
800 Acres

Recommended walk: Adams Point
Trail, 1 mile (loop), 1 hour

---

*A shoreline stretch along a scenic promontory of the Great
Bay tidal inlet.*

This inspiring walk follows part of the edge of Great
Bay, a tidal estuary of the Atlantic Ocean. With a fifty-
mile long shoreline, this inland estuary covers an
astounding 4,471 acres of open salt water, inlets,
marshes, and mudflats. Near Portsmouth the Piscataqua River feeds into Little Bay, which in turn
flows into Great Bay, creating a variety of salt marsh
and tidal creek wildlife environments. Expansive
scenic views of islands and inlets overtake ordinary
thoughts. The shimmer of light on the water and constant motion of the tides are overwhelming. Yet,
there's more to this walk than initially meets the eye.
Meadow, sea cliff, forest, and the lingering shades of a
bygone era entwine along this loop.

Enter the pass-through near a large old maple to
the right of the parking lot and walk down a path well
worn by students and professors from the nearby

A few Great Bay islands in the fifty-mile-long tidal estuary can be seen from the Adam's Point Trail.

University of New Hampshire. The trail is also popular with local fishermen and dog walkers. Cross a large open meadow dotted with sumac seedlings and a fair amount of poison ivy. The path, too, is lined with sumac, poison ivy, and thorny barberry shrubs. Side paths lead left onto the rocky shore, where you may wish to climb a bank to examine the knotted sea wrack with its air bladder floats, eastern slipper shells, and other organisms exposed at low tide.

With the meadow now on your right, walk along the shoreline beneath the shade of a row of oaks, shagbark hickory, and basswood (also called linden, a broad, ample tree with deeply furrowed bark and large, off-center heart-shaped leaves). Pass through an

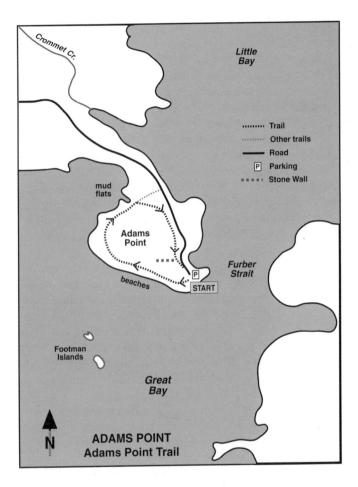

Legend:
- Trail
- Other trails
- Road
- P Parking
- Stone Wall

Crommet Cr.

Little Bay

mud flats

Adams Point

Furber Strait

P

START

beaches

Footman Islands

Great Bay

N

ADAMS POINT
Adams Point Trail

opening in a stone wall. This land once was a working farm and you'll see traces of farm equipment, cellar holes, and estate roads. Stone pasture walls, such as this one, are visible along the way.

Ascend a steep shale embankment through wind-stunted beech to taller hemlock and red pines. For a while, the trail follows the ridgeline of a 100-foot bluff above the gray rocky shale beach. Rock ledges jut out and form ideal balconies for scenic views of the islands and distant shores. Here the trail curves right with the point of land. Continue through a stand of birch and along the far side of the promontory, above a marshy area. Gulls and herons may be seen coasting the currents or hunting in the *Spartina* grass and tidal flats for shellfish.

The trail descends to sea level through clumps of white birch. Cross a plank bridge over a muddy back-water. Immediately after the bridge, you'll come to a junction. One branch of the trail continues straight, but turn right to loop back uphill through the woods. Where the trail levels, two tree trunks block the path. Notice, as you climb over them, the perfect round holes drilled by woodpeckers searching for insects burrowed in the rotted wood.

On the right now is a stone wall. On the left is the paved access road. Follow the trail, passing an abandoned rusty hayrack on your right, and cross through an opening in the stone wall.

This spot commands some interesting sights. Directly across the field, a white obelisk monument pokes above the weeds. Many New Hampshire farms such as this maintained their own family burial plots. Because of the abundant poison ivy here, we suggest you not venture over to investigate.

Just to your left, behind the stone wall, a rotund ancient hickory still bears nuts and provides shade for passersby. Turn left and walk close to the wall, keeping the meadow to your right. A chiseled granite foundation remains beneath the spreading taproots of a sumac grove.

You'll glimpse a marina prior to reentry past the maple sentinel at the gate and pass-through.

Getting There

From Durham take Route 108 south. Turn left onto Durham Point Road. Eventually it becomes Bay Road but isn't well marked. Drive 3.6 miles on this main paved road bordering Great Bay. On the left is a chain link gate with a large sign: "Gates Closed 10 P.M. to 4 A.M." Turn left past the gate and a mailbox labeled "Jackson Lab." Drive 0.5 mile down this access road, passing a large sign: "Adams Point Wilderness Management Area, New Hampshire Fish and Game Department." Continue another 0.5 mile on the access road to a parking lot at the Jackson Estuarine Laboratory.

Robert Frost Farm

Derry Village

100 Acres

Recommended walk: Hyla Brook Nature/
Poetry Trail, $1/2$ mile (loop), 1 hour

---

*A gentle ramble through the pasture, orchard, and birches
the famous Yankee poet once immortalized.*

A poet inextricably linked with New Hampshire,
Robert Frost (1874–1963) raised his family on this
farm. He kept five paths shoveled all winter for their
forays into the woods. The New Hampshire Division
of Parks and Recreation distributes a free informative
trail guide with excerpts of some of Frost's poems.
Numbers in the guide correspond to sites in the meadow, woodland, and Hyla Brook area. This pamphlet
and Frost memorabilia are kept in the barn near the
parking lot.

Begin the walk behind the white barn and where
the woods line the left edge of the field. Although trail
signs face the dark pine woods behind a stone wall,
numbers 1 through 8 in the guidebook actually correspond with plants and lore pertaining to the meadow
on your right.

Many of Frost's poems come to life as you stroll
along. Many are included in the trail guide, in addition to general commentary about his life and the site.

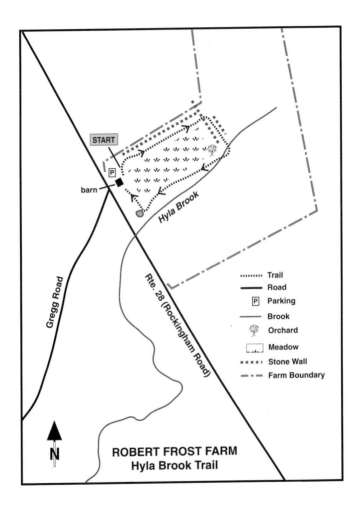

START

P

barn

Hyla Brook

Gregg Road

Rte. 28 (Rockingham Road)

Trail
Road
P Parking
Brook
Orchard
Meadow
Stone Wall
Farm Boundary

N

ROBERT FROST FARM
Hyla Brook Trail

A view of the meadow and barn at the Robert Frost Farm in Derry Village.

His poems "Pod of the Milkweed" and "Mowing," for instance, focus the walker's attention on the rolling field behind the farmhouse. Frost sold the farm in 1911 and by the 1950s the property had become an auto graveyard. Hundreds of car chassis had to be hauled away before new topsoil could be brought in to renew the low-cropped meadow you now see. Sweet fern, a shrub with frondlike leaves, still grows here as it did in Frost's time.

Continue through a break in the stone wall, then turn right onto a path in the woods. Lesley, Frost's eldest daughter, kept a journal with many references to woodchucks in the meadow. Her father's poem "A Drumlin Woodchuck" may have been inspired by her interest.

The moist meadow edges and brook areas on Frost's farm provided good ground for orchis, a variety of orchid. Growing from one to five feet high, the small lilac or white flowers in clusters on spikes inspired his poem "Quest of the Purple Fringed." Orchis still bloom here from June to August.

In carriage days of old, the path you're walking (numbers 10 to 13 in the guidebook) was Old South Road. It had a few houses on it but now only cellar holes remain.

Cross the small footbridge over Hyla Brook. According to Frost's poem of the same name, in early spring tiny tree frogs (genus *Hyla*), commonly known as "peepers," serenaded the Frost family. Their choruses resonate in ponds and bogs here and across New Hampshire in springtime.

Pass to your right down a few granite steps in an opening in the stone wall. For us this wall brought to mind "Mending Wall," one of Frost's most read poems. The poem relates how he and a neighbor met to rebuild walls after spring frost heaves had tumbled the stones onto each other's property. Frost wrote the poem in England, remembering how his Derry, New Hampshire, neighbor Napoleon Guay insisted on their traditional annual repair of the wall. Good fences made good neighbors. The importance of this effort was far from slight. Extraordinary labor went into clearing fields of stones the Ice Age glaciers had left.

Now cross a footbridge through a small stand of white pines and pass a few gnarled old apple trees.

Sixty young peach, pear, plum, and apple trees have been planted to replenish the original orchard.

Stations 20 through 23 are found along the opposite side of the meadow from where you started. You will pass through vetch, clover, Queen Anne's lace, and other meadow flowers.

Last time we visited the farm, the meadow already was mown for winter. However, in summer, a swath is cleared along the periphery through the tall grass. Walk toward the main road with the farmhouse, barn, and parking lot on your right.

Behind high shrubs on your left, a small mud pond greens in spring and summer, giving refuge to peepers, box turtles, and songbirds.

As a birder, botanist, and keen observer of nature, human and otherwise, venerable, tangy Robert Frost serves as the perfect guide for the unique sights and insights encountered on this walk. We hope other states will refer to this trail as a prototype for honoring poetry of and about the land.

Getting There

From Interstate 93 near Derry, take exit 4, then Route 102 north to Derry Village. At the rotary turn right on Route 28. The farm is 1.7 miles on your left.

Glossary

Boom log Linked tree trunks that float in front of dam outlets to prevent debris from clogging dam gates.

Buffer zone A semiwilderness area where humans and wildlife share common ground without infringement. A natural river park within an urban area is an example of an ecological buffer zone.

Cairn A rock-pile pyramid used to mark a trail.

Canopy The upper branches and crowns of a forest.

Clough quartzite White clumps of this metamorphic rock were deposited in New England by glacial activity and may be seen embedded in gneiss, shale, and other geological formations.

Conifers Also known as "softwoods," these trees have needles instead of leaves and are generally evergreen.

Deciduous trees Broad-leaved hardwoods that shed their leaves in the fall.

Deeryard Hemlock stands with thick branches provide shelter and protection for deer during heavy snows.

Duff Partly decayed leaves and pine needles on the forest floor.

Edge effects An area that forms a border between two or more habitats. These border habitats have a greater diversity of growth and offer protective cover for wildlife.

Emergent vegetation Plants with roots growing in lakes and riverbeds.

Field habitats "Old" fields (mowed every three to five years) enhance seed- and fruit-producing shrubs and plant life. "New" fields (mowed yearly) encourage the growth of annual grasses.

Flood-plain alluvium Overflow in the springtime creates these sedimentary deposits.

Glacial erratics Large boulders deposited by retreating glaciers during the Ice Age.

Gorse Spiny evergreens such as juniper and other prickly plants.

Ground cover Soil-hugging and retaining plants such as Canada mayflowers, creeping club moss, and moisture-loving partridgeberries.

Habitat An area characterized by certain plants and animals. For example, a meadow habitat supports a variety of wild grasses and flowers, which, in turn, support deer, rabbits, and other animals.

Intermittent stream A river that flows during the spring but dries up in summer.

Kettle holes When the glaciers retreated they left behind huge blocks of ice that formed large sinks in the earth. Glacial ponds.

Living cavity trees Dead standing trees (see Snags) make viable homes for a number of animals. The smaller hollows in tree trunks are used by birds, squirrels, and other wildlife for storing nuts, seeds, and berries.

Log landing A staging area for timber-hauling operations. Good wood-lot managers grade, fertilize, and seed these areas with grasses and clover between logging intervals. This practice controls erosion and protects natural water sources on the property.

Meander A turn or winding in a river.

Meander scar The river bend fills in with sediment so that only a trough is visible where water once flowed.

Mica Any group of silicates that crystallizes in fine transparent layers. New England isinglass (mica) was used to make wood and coal stove windows.

Monadnock A hill or mountain of resistant rock standing out on a peneplain. Grand Monadnock in southern New Hampshire is the prototype for this word.

Nesting boxes Man-made homes for cavity tree dwellers such as owls, squirrels, bluebirds.

Northern Tooth An inedible layered shelf fungus that feeds on the heartwood of sugar maples and other hardwoods. It is best to remove the fungus as it weakens the tree.

Outwash plain Several thousand years ago, glacial waters spread debris and deposited soil of gravel and sand, sometimes many yards deep.

Oxbow A U-shaped bend is created when the river current cuts one bank faster and deeper than the other. Eventually the bend is cut off by the sediment deposits and an oxbow lake forms.

Samara The winged seedpods of maples.

Seep Groundwater that percolates to the surface. Seeps create foraging patches and drinking holes for animals in winter.

Selective cutting A forest management practice in which some trees are chosen for cutting to allow clearings in understory, thus opening the forest to successional growth.

Snags Dead standing trees. Insect cities thrive in the rotting bark. Birds and animals live in the cavities of these trees. These trees can, however, pose a danger to hikers during times of high wind.

Succession communities Each level of vegetation makes way for the next. Perennial weeds are replaced by fruit-bearing plants and small shrubs. These, in turn, are replaced by small trees. Finally, the small trees give way to taller shade trees.

Talus Rock debris at the base of cliffs and mountain slopes.

Tannin Organic substances, such as pine needles, that dye freshwater streams and ponds brown.

Tree girdling Forest managers cut rings in the bark around the trunks of certain trees. The tree then dies but is left standing for nesting birds and animals.

Tree line The division between forest and rocky, open summit.

Tree release To increase the production of wild fruit and nut trees, neighboring shade trees are pruned.

Understory The layer of forest beneath the canopy, the growth area from the forest floor to the lower tree branches.

Vernal pools Snowmelt and rain, in spring, form small puddles on the forest floor. These pools form sites for amphibian breeding because fish predators are absent.

Watershed A drainage area for any body of water.

Wetlands Ponds, marshes, backwaters of streams, tidal estuaries, sinks, bogs, and other bodies of water that form invaluable habitats for wildlife and plant life.

Wolf trees Beech, oak, and hickory with superabundant supplies of seeds and nuts.

About the AMC

THE Appalachian Mountain Club pursues a vigorous conservation agenda while encouraging responsible recreation, based on the philosophy that successful, long-term conservation depends upon first-hand experience of the natural environment. More than 64,000 members have joined the AMC to pursue their interests in hiking, canoeing, skiing, walking, rock climbing, bicycling, camping, kayaking, and backpacking, and—at the same time—to help safeguard the environment in which these activities are possible.

Since it was founded in 1876, the Club has been at the forefront of the environmental protection movement. By cofounding several of New England's leading environmental organizations, and working in coalition with these and many more groups, the AMC has positively influenced legislation and public opinion.

Volunteers in each chapter lead hundreds of outdoor activities and excursions and offer introductory instruction in backcountry sports. The AMC education department offers members and the public a wide range of workshops, from introductory camping to the intensive Mountain Leadership School taught on the trails of the White Mountains.

The most recent efforts in the AMC conservation program include river protection, Northern Forest

Lands policy, Sterling Forest (NY) preservation, and support for the Clean Air Act.

The AMC's research department focuses on the forces affecting the ecosystem, including ozone levels, acid rain and fog, climate change, rare flora and habitat protection, and air quality and visibility.

The AMC trails program maintains over 1,400 miles of trail (including 350 miles of the Appalachian Trail) and more than 50 shelters in the Northeast. Through a coordinated effort of volunteers, seasonal crews, and program staff, the AMC contributes more than 10,000 hours of public service work each summer in the area from Washington, D.C. to Maine.

The club operates eight alpine huts in the White Mountains that provide shelter, bunks and blankets, and hearty meals for hikers. Pinkham Notch Visitor Center, at the foot of Mt. Washington, is base camp to the adventurous and the ideal location for individuals and families new to outdoor recreation. For reservations, call 603-466-2727.

At the AMC headquarters in Boston and at Pinkham Notch Visitor Center in New Hampshire, the bookstore and information center stock the entire line of AMC publications, as well as other trail and river guides, maps, reference materials, and the latest articles on conservation issues. Guidebooks and other AMC gifts are available by mail order (AMC, P.O. Box 298, Gorham NH 03581), or call toll-free 800-262-4455. Also available from the bookstore or by subscription is *Appalachia*, the country's oldest mountaineering and conservation journal.

Alphabetical Listing of Areas